Manipulating Meetings

Yor

D0470084

About the author

DAVID MARTIN FCIS, FIPD, is a well-known author of over 25 business titles, including *Tough Talking, Tough Telephoning*, and *Dealing with Demanding Customers* as well as *The Company Directors Desktop Guide* (Hawksmere) and several titles for the Chartered Institute of Secretaries series of *One Stop* books. He has run his own consultancy, Buddenbrook, for over 15 years carrying out various projects in the corporate communications, personnel management and related areas. He gives up to 100 seminars on such subjects each year. He is consultant editor of Tolley's *Essential Business Facts* and author-editor of Gee's *Employment letters and procedures, Model employment policies and handbooks* and *Discipline, dismissal and redundancy*. He sits on the Registrar of Companies wider users committee and is a CBI member of the Employment Tribunals panel.

The Institute of Management (IM) is at the forefront of management development and best management practice. The Institute embraces all levels of management from students to chief executives. It provides a unique portfolio of services for all managers, enabling them to develop skills and achieve management excellence.

If you would like to hear more about the benefits of membership, please write to Department P, Institute of Management, Cottingham Road, Corby NN17 1TT.

This series is commissioned by the Institute of Management Foundation.

SMARTER SOLUTIONS

The performance pack

Manipulating Meetings

How to get what you want, when you want it

DAVID MARTIN

Prentice Hall

London · New York · Toronto · Sydney · Tokyo · Singapore
Madrid · Mexico City · Munich · Paris

YORK COLLEGE

STAMPED✗ CAT. MℒC

ACC. No. 065499

CLASS No. 658.456 MAR

LEARNING RESOURCES
CENTRE

PEARSON EDUCATION LIMITED

Head Office:
Edinburgh Gate
Harlow CM20 2JE
Tel: +44 (0)1279 623623
Fax: +44 (0)1279 431059

London Office:
128 Long Acre
London WC2E 9AN
Tel: +44 (0)207 447 2000
Fax: +44 (0)207 240 5771
www.business-minds.com

First published in Great Britain 1996

© David Martin 2000

The right of David Martin to be identified as Author of this Work has been asserted by him in accordance with the Copyright, Designs, and Patents Act 1988.

ISBN 0 273 64500 5

British Library Cataloguing in Publication Data
A CIP catalogue record for this book can be obtained from the British Library.

All rights reserved; no part of this publication may be reproduced, stored in a retrieval system, or transmitted in any form or by any means, electronic, mechanical, photocopying, recording, or otherwise without either the prior written permission of the Publishers or a licence permitting restricted copying in the United Kingdom issued by the Copyright Licensing Agency Ltd, 90 Tottenham Court Road, London W1P 0LP. This book may not be lent, resold, hired out or otherwise disposed of by way of trade in any form of binding or cover other than that in which it is published, without the prior consent of the Publishers.

10 9 8 7 6 5 4 3 2 1

Typeset by Northern Phototypesetting Co. Ltd, Bolton
Printed and bound in Great Britain by Biddles Ltd, Guildford and King's Lynn

The Publishers' policy is to use paper manufactured from sustainable forests.

Contents

CONTENTS

Introduction

The idea for *Manipulating Meetings* came from a reference incorporated in its best selling predecessor *Tough Talking*. The theme of *Tough Talking* is that to win in negotiating situations it is essential to determine our desired result and that very often we lose encounters simply because we do not identify what our desired result is and fail to steer the encounter to the achievement of that aim.

In running meetings there is a similar challenge – to achieve the purpose of the meeting, and an equally similar failure rate simply because often we do not prepare or prepare adequately and take time to consider how best to achieve what we want. Manipulation is an emotive word suggesting devious behaviour or underhand activity usually engaged upon by those with Machiavellian tendencies. However, as a company secretary who has spent a great deal of his working life in all sorts of meetings, from successful to disastrous, I would argue that by manipulating meetings and meeting members, sometimes gently and invisibly and sometimes not so gently and with a high profile, it is possible to attain the aims – and attain them more effectively and efficiently than is often the case.

Putting Machiavellian tendencies to one side, my prime purpose is to examine ways and means by which those responsible for meetings (which if unstructured can consume or, more bluntly, waste an enormous amount of management time) can ensure that their legitimate ends are attained. Very often this can be achieved by basic items such as improving preparation, planning for eventualities and ensuring efficiency – those often overlooked but invaluable administrative aids. At other times, however, far more draconian measures are essential if the organisation is to move forward. Meetings are endemic in every aspect of human life. Most of these tend to be one-to-one face-to-face meetings, 'the best meeting' as it is suggested here. In business, however, the propensity for multi-member meetings increases considerably – indeed employees of some organisations seem to spend much of their working lives within them.

'Manipulation' in that environment can be as much about avoiding meetings as about ensuring their effective operation and decision-making process. Too often such meetings are used as excuses to delay or defer action or as a means of avoiding accountability. It is arguable that in considering holding a meeting:

- requirements should be challenged to ensure real need

- convening should be controlled to ensure real discussion and

- conduct should be contrived to achieve decisions in accordance with aims and purpose.

Manipulation is double-edged, it can help you attain your aims, but can also be employed by others to frustrate those aims, whilst helping them attain theirs. To help negate the impact of such actions, a number of defensive techniques have also been included.

Much of the success of both *Tough Talking* and *Manipulating Meetings* has been derived from their user-friendly presentation and in particular their use of real-life and practical case studies to illustrate theory. *Tough Talking* explores the problems of business relationships in general and suggests ways in which the conflict that arises during such interfacing can be avoided or resolved. *Manipulating Meetings* relates the same approach but it is directed purely at improving the practice of meetings. Both titles, as well as the third in the series, *Dealing with Demanding Customers*, emphasise heavily the point that often merely the failure to set and remember the 'desired result', from which all our actions, manipulations and defences should follow, can mean we fail in our endeavour.

David M. Martin, Buddenbrook
November 1999

CHAPTER ONE

Is your meeting really necessary?

Key learning points

■ Essential to assess meetings' resource usage to ensure they are cost-effective

■ Examine, and re-examine, the requirement for a meeting and hold only those with 'meat'

■ Appreciate that the results of meetings can be attained via other formats

■ Meetings can reduce accountability and delay decision taking

■ Policies, procedures and checklists can be used to render some meetings unnecessary

---

'Meetings take minutes and waste hours' runs an old saying and if this is true of meetings in which you or your organisation become involved then remedial action is needed. Such action may be as simple as ensuring that meetings' aims are clarified and promulgated and that all participants are constantly reminded of and brought back to the task of attaining such aims. However, that is already accepting the inevitability of the need to hold the meeting in the first place which may be a false assumption. Thus before dealing with result we should consider the cause. In other words:

- before agreeing to hold a meeting we should challenge its very existence
- before discovering how to use and manipulate meetings to serve their, or our, purpose, we should consider alternative, and possibly more cost-effective, ways of achieving the same end
- before learning how to deal with awkward meeting members and how to combat their machinations we should consider ways of circumventing their actions in advance.

The cost examination

A very cursory and crude examination of the time and money invested in meetings demonstrates the potential advantage of considering alternative means of solving problems. In every organisation, since all should be concerned to maximise the use of resources, it should be obvious that every item of expenditure needs to be examined, and re-examined, regularly. The considerable time that management and others may spend in meetings should be no exception to such an examination. The acid test (Fig. 1.1) can be applied to all meetings.

---

a) Total the salaries or wages of all involved in the meeting and add 25-40 per cent for the payroll and all applicable oncosts. Reduce this to a cost per working minute. If there are 260 working days in a year and 7 working hours in a day, this divisor will be 109,200.

b) Calculate the duration of the meeting in minutes.

c) Multiply (a) by (b) to find a 'meeting time cost'.

d) List the decision results attained by the meeting. Produce the above workings to the Chairman and query whether the decision results were worth the meeting time cost.

Figure 1.1 The acid test of meetings

This is a somewhat tongue in cheek analysis, but nevertheless analysis of the 'time cost' of meetings should not just focus attention on the need for greater account-ability, but also raise the question 'was your meeting really necessary?' The ultimate question must be 'is there a way of dealing with the problem without needing to convene a meeting?'

Meetings without 'meat'

Before agreeing to a meeting the question 'is this meeting really necessary?' should be posed, and posed not just for the initial meeting but regularly thereafter.

CASE STUDY 1.1   **What's the point?**

The committee set up to run a social club had originated and gained approval for a constitution, found premises and sourced a working leader. In appointing the latter, virtually all the duties and responsibilities formerly undertaken by the committee were transferred to him, nevertheless the committee continued to meet. Virtually to justify its existence, it then required the leader to report to it each month, even though all the meeting members were involved as club members and knew every development.

──────── KEY TECHNIQUE ────────

The original purpose of the committee had been exhausted, but until this was realised it continued to meet.

───────────────────────────────

Since experience shows that a large number of purposeless meetings or 'meetings without meat' are held, one objective of challenging the existence of all such meetings should be to ensure that each does have sufficient 'meat', and indeed 'meat' of the correct flavour, to warrant convening or continuation. Sadly meetings are often held:

a) lacking any real purpose but simply because it is either a matter of habit or is an easy way out of the decision-making process

b) for the wrong reason(s) which will automatically generate the wrong decisions

c) as a method of shifting responsibility from an individual to a collective basis (*Note:* since there is a widespread tendency to promote above the level of incompetence – the Peter Principle – which results in managers being expected to operate at one level above that for which their talents and experience suit them, this may

3

encourage over-promoted managers to protect their positions by seeking a meeting to take responsibility for decisions which are properly their own)

d) as a delaying or spoiling tactic. If a swift decision is essential for the success of the project, deferral to a meeting may either kill it off, or ensure that its success is marred or rendered impossible or

e) as a means of achieving a 'hidden agenda', that is moving towards a decision which has an effect additional to those visible and recognised by most people.

The meeting syndrome

In meeting-orientated organisations, decision delays can occur because they are not taken until everyone can fit a meeting into their schedules, which may be congested simply because of the sheer number of meetings! In addition, because decisions are usually taken in meetings or after discussion in meetings, decision makers or managers may become timid, afraid to take decisions in their own name.

CASE STUDY 1.2　　　　**Too much too late from too many**

As an inexperienced manager in my first executive position I remember being given, on my first day in a new job, a job description which included the requirement to obtain references for proposed new employees from their previous employers for fidelity guarantee insurance cover. My predecessor's files were haphazard and I could not understand the procedure followed. On contacting the Personnel Department for help, I was told 'oh we must have a meeting about that', which was set for two days later. This meeting, involving no less than eight people was informative in terms of getting to know the people involved and, as a result of the advice provided in a somewhat haphazard way, a procedure was developed which solved the problem. However this could have been achieved in a ten-minute, two-party, face-to-face chat two days earlier, rather than an hour-long multi-member meeting.

──────── KEY TECHNIQUE ────────

Whilst the meeting may well have been successful in terms of building a working relationship, in terms of its real purpose, immediate guidance of a newcomer in an unclear procedure, the meeting failed. The two or three day delay in chasing up references from former employers could have resulted in an unsuitable applicant being offered employment.

What is a meeting?

One dictionary defines a meeting as 'an encounter, public gathering of people for a purpose', whilst another defines it as 'an assembly of people for discussion'. If these are the best definitions of meetings, at least in business terms, and are used as guides by conveners and participants, then it is hardly surprising that so many meetings are ineffective. In attempting to provide a framework within which we can ensure we get the most from meetings, we need a more closely focused definition. This can possibly utilise extracts from both the above but must incorporate two essential ingredients that neither of the two definitions addresses – the need for a meeting to have both purpose and aim.

Meetings – a new definition

A gathering of essential participants only, each of whom has something to contribute, to discuss a problem touching on all their interests, to arrive at certain decisions, all as required by the pre-determined aim of the meeting itself.

This is obviously a far lengthier definition than perhaps space allowed either of my dictionaries to incorporate, but does, by including elements of control dynamism and purpose, set parameters within which we can work towards convening an effective meeting.

Avoiding meetings

The number one rule in developing an approach to meetings may be to avoid them if possible, and to restrict them if not. This is not to say that all meetings are unnecessary. Many are essential and the organisation's work could not be attained without them. However, very often multi-delegate meetings are held for the most specious and unnecessary reasons. Whether the organisation can, or will, reduce the number of meetings held, will however depend very much on its ethos. There may be little point attempting to reduce the number of meetings in an organisation where most of the main players and the system is very committed to holding meetings and extending their coverage, although there are instances where new Managing Directors have succeeded in doing just that. In most organisations, however, the number of meetings indulged in can be severely reduced by positive and constant commitment to furthering decision making swiftly and economically in other ways, only agreeing to a meeting once aim and purpose have been set and other alternatives have been examined.

Meeting alternatives

To initiate action, an instigator needs to obtain a reaction from a target. This can be achieved in at least two ways, either by giving instructions, that is following a 'sole person' decision, or by discussing requirements leading to an agreement of what is needed, that is a joint 'interested parties' decision. Both can be effective, but their use must be assessed on each occasion, since they need to be employed in different situations.

CASE STUDY 1.3 **Security requirements – 1**

The factory had been subject to a number of petty thefts. It was pointed out that leaving the unmanned main gates open after the end of a shift, so that those working overtime could walk directly to the car park rather than taking a short detour via a manned alternative exit, was an invitation to thieves to sneak into the premises. The Director took the decision that these gates would in future be closed ten minutes after the normal shift ended. A note was given to all employees explaining the decision, why it had been taken, and when it would come into effect.

──────── KEY TECHNIQUE ────────

It is arguable that a meeting of all employees or their representatives could have been called, the problem discussed and the proposals debated. It is doubtful if the decision would have been any different, and meanwhile the thefts could have continued.

CASE STUDY 1.4   **Security requirements – 2**

The problems of theft, outlined in the previous case study, abated but losses continued. Accordingly, the Director decided that the right to carry out random searches of employees was necessary. He convened a meeting of union representatives to discuss the problem and agree a course of action. After considerable discussion and amendment of detail, the proposals were put into effect with active Union support.

———— KEY TECHNIQUE ————

Had the Director tried to implement the second decision by decree rather than by consultation, without involving employee representatives and discussing the problem and alternative solutions, the potential backlash could have been considerable. Investing resources in the meeting saved potential resource wastage in the event of disagreement.

Communication is not information

Whether they be effective or ineffective, or made in or out of meetings, all decisions revolve around a need for communication. Unless such communication is effective it may be impossible to resolve anything. Unfortunately the true nature of communication, which is essential in all human life, let alone in economic endeavour, is often misunderstood or confused. Nowhere is this more true than in an interface between just two participants, and if communication can be misunderstood between just two players imagine how much greater is the capacity for misunderstanding when there are a greater number of players.

If A meets B and tells him that the production target for this week is 1000 widgets he may feel he is communicating with B. But this is not so, he is merely informing. Although information is essential, in no way does it involve B, or gain any commitment from him. However, if A has a meeting with B, asks him what manpower he has available, whether there are adequate supplies of raw material and power, and whether there are any problems in attaining the week's production target, he has begun the communication process. If he then actively listens to, not passively 'hears', the answers, which may themselves include problems requiring solution, and then A and B jointly decide a course of action, communication is in process and is helping to attain the joint ends of the participants' meeting. True communication consists of a meeting of minds and a gaining of consensus. It is essentially a two-way dialogue involving comprehension of both parties' viewpoints, concerns and priorities, which can only be achieved by an **exchange** of information and feedback. It is a dynamic, not a passive, process affecting all parties as is shown in Fig. 1.2.

Sender	I	F		C	
Data encoded	N	E		O	
Transmitted	F	E		M	
Received	O	D		M	
Decoded	R	B		U	
	M	A		N	
	A	C		I	
	T	K		C	
Recipient	I			A	
Received	O			T	
Decoded	N			I	
Comprehension				O	
Clarification				N	

Figure 1.2   Information does not equal communication
(from the author's *How to control your costs and increase your profits*)

Self-perpetuating meetings

The importance of differentiating between information and communication cannot be overestimated not just in deciding which is appropriate in order to avoid investing resources in a meeting, but also, if avoidance is impossible, in manipulating members, individuals and alliances, as well as the meeting itself. Whilst a meeting may be required to determine policy or changes to policy, in which case an interplay of different views and queries may be essential, there is often a great deal which is actually no more than a review of the status quo, requiring little or no input from members who are required only to note and digest. The problem is that the scenario in which meeting members find themselves, actually pressurises them to comment or question data or decisions simply to justify their presence. Indeed, this can hold true even though the subject matter may be provided purely for information, and their comments are virtually irrelevant. In these circumstances, such comments may be only serving the purpose of prolonging a redundant meeting.

CASE STUDY 1.5   **No need to comment**

The Secretary was required to update the Board on developments on rent reviews of a number of the company's leased properties. In view of the large number of such properties this meant that at any time he would need to report on around twenty negotiations. Very often most of the factors that would dictate a new level were outside the control of the company and, whilst his brief was to achieve as low an increase as possible, market forces tended to militate against this and the company had ultimately to accept the almost inevitable increases. This agenda item began to consume between 30 and 45 minutes, until he decided to include, as part of the agenda, a synopsis of the status of each negotiation, and suggested to the Chairman that discussion only take place on an 'exception basis', that is that discussion was only invited where there were particular factors or facts of relevance that were perceived to have been overlooked, the remainder being an information exercise only. Thereafter, not only did the members have a written and detailed update, rather than a verbal report, but also the time devoted to the item dropped to 10 minutes or so.

——— KEY TECHNIQUE ———

Advance single member research may enable the meeting's attention to be concentrated on the essentials.

Making the meeting redundant

The process developed in Case Study 1.5 was later adopted for a number of other routine reports so that the 'discussion aspect' of those items was removed. This process can be used with other business that is often referred to a meeting for noting rather than decision. Similarly, originating procedures and checklists for policy matters will provide guidance for those required to implement decisions rather than needing Board approval on each occasion.

CASE STUDY 1.6   **In accordance with policy …**

The company was concerned that a number of its long-serving employees were retiring without income, other than the state pension, as, due to a formerly restricted entry requirement, they had not been able to join the occupational pension scheme. Accordingly, during a number of Board meetings a policy and a procedure for granting *ex gratia* allowances to such employees was agreed and a number of cases examined. Thereafter, however, the Personnel Department automatically calculated the entitlement and set up the payment, under a Director's authorisation. Each year the Board continued to review the system, but from a policy, not an administrative, angle.

———— KEY TECHNIQUE ————

Developing policies and procedures, checklists and guidance not only avoids the need for meetings to discuss individual cases, but also provides ongoing guidance to those who need to make decisions. The availability of criteria and checklists can negate the need for repeated discussions and should also avoid one-off solutions that may create unwanted precedents.

Backlash

Obviously reducing discussion to 'exception only' reporting may not please everyone. Some meeting members regard their membership and attendance as enhancing their prestige and position, and the length of the meeting as indicative of its, and, by reflection, their, importance. Removing routine business restricts their capacity for comment on non-essentials where they are unlikely to say the 'wrong thing'. If they cannot comment on such mundane items, then their total contribution to the meeting may be, and be seen to be, limited, which may, in turn, question their continued membership. Contributions should be examined in case the number of meeting members can be reduced which may, in turn, reduce the duration of the meeting.

Role specifications

In addition to creating policy documents, strict delineation of job roles and specifications should also assist in avoiding or reducing meetings, whether these be of the 'one-to-one' or 'multi-member' variety. Often meeting members find themselves involved in sorting out responsibilities or needing to reconcile differing interpretations of their roles and duties. Clarification of each department's role and each employee's responsibilities and job requirements by means of specifications and job descriptions, should avoid the waste of meeting time.

CASE STUDY 1.7   **Not my job ...**

At the first meeting of a new committee the Chairman called for detailed production figures and was greeted first by a loud silence and then, as he investigated, by recriminations and accusations from two or three of the members present, each of whom insisted that responsibility for the production of the statistics rested with another party. No job descriptions were used in the company and thus the question of whose responsibility it was, became a source of unprofitable debate.

──────── KEY TECHNIQUE ────────

Delineation of authority as well as the inclusion of measures of performance in job and departmental specifications can help reduce meeting time spent on routine matters. Measures of performance provide an agreed criteria against which accountability can be assessed.

Discipline and absence

In considering areas where there seems to be considerable scope for dissent leading to meetings, we should not overlook disciplinary and absence problems. Once again, both incidence and time involved will be exaggerated if the expectations of the organisation have not been clearly explained. Setting out clear examples of behaviour which will lead to the application of the disciplinary procedure puts employees on notice as to what is and what is not expected of them. Subsequent breaches of the requirements can then be dealt with in accordance with the procedure, avoiding the discussions over what is or is not permitted. Similarly, adopting a procedure for dealing with malingerers, or even the long-term genuinely sick, and promulgating it to all concerned, means that those affected know from the outset what attitudes and investigations will be implemented should they 'offend'. Thus the propensity to challenge the organisation's actions in a meeting, and their incidence, should be restricted.

Monitoring progress between meetings

Wastage of time in a series of meetings tends to be endemic as meeting members fall into habits. Forcing routine business out of the meeting and requiring comment only on an exception basis may restrict such wastage. However, in addition, the following up of required action between meetings and requesting updates prior to the meeting, rather than at it, may also assist. If such updates are distributed with the agenda, this will also provide thinking time in advance of the meeting rather than utilising the meeting time itself for this purpose.

Forcing a meeting

The suggestions made here are that business and required decisions should be manipulated in order either to avoid meetings, or to reduce the time required to be invested in them. The result of such a commitment should be not just that the overall number of meetings is reduced, but also that those meetings that do take place concentrate on essential business only. This does not mean that meetings should be avoided or evaded at all costs or that time is the ultimate criterion for effectiveness. On occasion the holding of a meeting with a definite purpose can be extremely beneficial and may even save the time and the use of alternative resources. The decision-making process can take several forms, and one or more means of solution may be acceptable. What is required on every occasion is the commitment to an objective assessment of what the best solution is likely to be, rather than an automatic assumption that a meeting is required.

CASE STUDY 1.8 **Meeting better than writing**

A customer had a major query with a company's product and service and had written to the local outlet to gain information and redress. Inadequate and insufficient explanations had been provided and thus the customer involved the Head Office at Board level. As a result a three-way correspondence ensued which went on for several weeks and, even after compensation was paid, left the customer feeling that he had been inefficiently and poorly treated. In terms of customer care this was hardly an encouraging outcome, whilst in terms of potential adverse publicity it was dangerous. A meeting between the customer and a senior person in the company, who could have explained the problem and ensured proper restitution, might have achieved a better and swifter solution.

———— KEY TECHNIQUE ————

In this instance a meeting would have had the advantage of a recognition of body language, was unlikely to have degenerated into dispute and would have had the additional advantage of not providing a written record of the maladministration. The time invested in a meeting would have avoided the potential downside as well as the resources consumed in a lengthy and at times acrimonious correspondence.

Unfortunately these kinds of defensive 'maintain our position at all costs' arguments are far too numerous. Written communications lack eye and voice expression (indeed they lack all body language) and we use language which may have different and unwanted meanings to different people which can create or compound misunderstandings – one cannot ask questions of, or seek elucidation from, a piece of paper. In physical meetings one can use body language to 'soften' arguments and counterings – even the tone we use can be all important. Whilst recommending that organisations should try to reduce meetings, it would be counter-productive if they were then to be replaced by a 'memo paper chase' where decisions and discussions can only be effected via written claim and counter-claims. Not only is this a long-winded and tedious approach, it also tends to be even more costly. Realism and objectivity is essential and should be constant.

CHAPTER TWO

So you do need a meeting

Key learning points

■ Assess the nature of and then convene the most appropriate meeting for the task

■ Consider the implications of the format of the meeting chosen, and prepare accordingly

■ Preparation and planning outside the meeting should lay a foundation for achieving a desired result in the meeting

■ Electronically connected meetings can save time and money but possibly at the expense of rapport and understanding

What kind of meeting

There are several types of meeting and, whilst it is important to avoid the incidence of 'meetings without meat', it is equally important, should a meeting need to be held, that it is suitable for the purpose.

Types of meeting

1 **Face to face.** This involves two parties coming together either by mutual design at a pre-set time, or by deliberate design of one of them waylaying the other, or by an unplanned encounter at which they take the opportunity to discuss business. The principles of the two-party meeting are developed in greater detail in Chapter 3.

2 **Impromptu informal gathering.** This is usually set in action by, say, a senior person suggesting that a few interested parties 'get together and thrash out a solution'.

3 **Brainstorming.** This is a development of the impromptu informal gathering and can be very effective particularly where the aim is the development of creative ideas which, by their very nature are innovative and which, in order to 'flow', require interaction with, as well as reaction from, others.

4 *Ad hoc* **committee.** This has similarities with the 'impromptu informal gathering' although it will normally be more structured to the extent of having an agenda and probably a pre-set time. The concept allows time for advance thought. Such meetings tend to be informal and may be productive. As the level of formality increases the time committed to the meeting tends to increase, usually at the expense of productivity.

5 **Regular committee.** This description covers a wide range of meetings often given other titles, for example, executive, board, and so on. These tend to create a formality of their own and to be pre-planned some time in advance. They may also be described as standing committees, that is they have a continuing role as opposed to the *ad hoc* single-subject role. As such, these meetings tend to consider standard business for the most part but with *ad hoc* business, which may be of quite a wide-ranging nature, included irregularly.

6 **Formal meeting.** These meetings tend to deal mainly with routine and non-controversial matters and may provide final authority for decisions possibly hammered out at a meeting with subordinate authority. Whilst there are some overtones of the 'rubber stamp' type of body, this can be dramatically changed if controversial matters need decisions.

7 **Presentations.** In this format the participants tend to resemble the teacher–pupil relationship rather than delegates with more or less equal stature. The format needs careful handling by the presenter to avoid disruptive elements wasting delegates' time. Presentations are dealt with in Chapter 14.

8 **Public meetings.** Again the word 'meeting' is being somewhat misconstrued here since the normal purpose is for the instigator to use the opportunity to deliver a point of view or information, not necessarily to generate reaction.

Tactics

Each of these meetings requires its own approach, and we should be able to maximise the use of the meeting by considering our attitude and devising appropriate tactics in advance.

Impromptu informal

The problem for the members is that they will be caught unawares with little time to consider the subject matter whilst the urgency and enthusiasm of the instigator may be difficult to resist, particularly if he is senior to them. Because the meeting is convened in a rush its purpose may be unfocused and unclear. There is thus a danger of it taking far more time than is necessary, since the questions and arguments of each participant will be enunciated in an unstructured way reflecting their lack of preparation. This can be compounded if the instigator himself is someone who acts on instinct and has set up the meeting with insufficient thought and planning. In this instance the arguments and pressure of the instigator may themselves take time to crystallise, the discussion thus becoming circular rather than progressive. In being diverted from other work, the participants' effectiveness may be considerably impaired. Although difficult to resist, if history demonstrates that such meetings tend to be less than effective, participants may need (a) to find out the subject matter swiftly and (b) to attempt to delay the 'immediacy' of the gathering to allow some thinking time.

CASE STUDY 2.1 **Curbing the Chairman – 1**

The Chairman was a dynamic and restless, but highly creative, individual who was able to generate an apparently endless stream of new ideas. Some of these ideas were highly successful, others were not. Such was his enthusiasm, it was difficult to avoid spending considerable time challenging the less successful notions until he either tired of the idea, thought of something else or realised himself that it wasn't such a good idea after all. He operated with a small team based at Head Office but spent much of his time with the several operational units throughout the United Kingdom. Since he was fond of the impromptu gathering, his Head

▶

▶

Office executives arranged with their contacts in the operating units that, if they realised that another 'bright idea' had just dawned, they would tip them off. On one occasion the tip-off came with the added news that the Chairman was driving straight back to Head Office with the aim of holding an immediate meeting to discuss implementation. The team swiftly arranged alternative meetings themselves away from the office so that they would not be available on his arrival. Their, perhaps cavalier, action was vindicated when within 24 hours the 'bright idea' in question was shown to be valueless and swiftly and quietly dropped.

———— KEY TECHNIQUE ————

The trouble with bright ideas, and particularly with apparently original ideas, is that often they are not original at all and may have already been discarded for good, but perhaps not obvious, reasons, which a little thought and preparation time might well have disclosed. Holding discussion meetings in such circumstances merely consumes resources.

Brainstorming

These are both meeting and meeting-avoidance tactics in one. After all if a meeting seems inevitable, for example to deal with the subject of the impromptu gathering referred to above, it may be possible to suggest instead that the participants hold a brainstorming session lasting, say, not more than 30 minutes. At least in this way their time investment is being controlled – provided of course that the time limit is strictly applied. The principle of cutting short discussion is not restricted to brainstorming sessions, but can be used to restrict the duration of more formal meetings.

A danger with brainstorming sessions, common to other meetings, is that they can be hijacked by the articulate or self-assured to the detriment of those less able to express themselves although possessed of valuable and original thought. This places an onus on the leader or Chairman to ensure the full participation of all present, curbing the excesses of some and encouraging others. Conversely, should the Chairman's own preferences veer towards the opinion of the articulate members, then there may be a tendency 'not to hear' any opposition. Thus the Chairman will be manipulating the meeting, and, although those opposing may be able to muster an attack and make their points known, if the Chairman is not in favour of their views, it may be difficult to win the arguments, and further, impossible, without the Chairman's support, to succeed in any implementation. Having said that, Chairmen do not always win discussions.

CASE STUDY 2.2 **Curbing the Chairman – 2**

The Chairman was a very strong personality: 'an ideal leader but not always an ideal businessman', as one of his colleagues once described him. Although always very strong on ensuring that high achieving employees were well rewarded, he was not averse to making sure that his own position was equally well rewarded. With the approach of his retirement however, he realised that his control over the annual pension review would disappear and so he endeavoured to gain the ongoing commitment of the Board, whilst still Chairman, to a large annual increase, in the payment of which, of course, he had a vested interest. Two of his colleagues, whilst not wishing to cause Board dissent immediately prior to his retirement, combined forces to ensure that the future Board was not saddled with such a liability. Faced with their tactful but firm opposition, the Chairman backed away from the confrontation.

———— KEY TECHNIQUE ————

Alliances can help resist the hijacking of the meeting's aims in favour of a member's personal aims.

Ad hoc committee

The purpose of such a committee is to consider specific business. That being so, those appointed should be given not only detailed terms of reference but also a time by which their conclusions and recommendations should be reported. If these controls are not installed, the deliberations of the committee can be unnecessarily extended by members. This can be true of some political committees, particularly where there is scope for foreign travel and so on, which will be paid for from the public purse. Strict terms of reference, linked to a budget, should be framed. In addition, only those really qualified to consider the subject matter should be appointed, as supernumeraries will not only extend the deliberations but may also blunt the effectiveness of the appointees whose work has value.

Regular committee

This type of meeting is to be found in most organisations. Such widespread use should not generate complacency regarding its effectiveness. Like every other meeting it needs controlling in order to be effective although the fact that regular business is required to be considered may exert a control of its own. A strong Chairman is required in order to ensure the ends or aims of the meeting are achieved within a reasonable timeframe. In part this may be achieved by referring suitable business to sub-committees which are required to 'report back'. The main meeting needs only to consider business on an 'exception basis'.

If sub-committees are not used and the Chairman allows too much debate on items, the meeting's duration will tend to expand. This can be countered by devices such as:

- the *guillotine* or *cloture*, that is cutting short the meeting by setting an overall time limit. The guillotine was first used around 1910 to ensure progress through the House of Commons of certain finance acts, but the cloture (or closure) predates it, having been introduced in Parliament in 1882. It can be applied only when supported by at least 100 votes

- the *kangaroo*, that is cutting short discussion on a particular point by requiring a decision after a set time and then moving to the next business

- *standing*. Since the meetings of the UK Privy Council in the nineteenth century tended to take a considerable amount of time, the custom, which continues to the present day, was developed for, or at the instigation of, Queen Victoria of holding the meetings with all participants (except presumably the Queen herself) standing. The uncomfortableness of the position concentrated the mind on the meeting's priorities and reduced its duration! Interestingly, some organisations in Australia use a similar idea with chest-high desks and no chairs in meeting rooms to ensure short meetings.

Obviously time is not necessarily a sound criterion for a meeting's effectiveness and forcing a meeting to end swiftly when there is business requiring considered attention is as poor management of resources as convening a meeting without 'meat'.

External meetings

Most of the meetings referred to in this book are internal with all members working for the same organisation. Although internal politics will play a role, this can be controlled by the Chairman and even countered by members themselves. Should one, or more, members indulge in political activity the most effective response may be to highlight it. A terse 'now come on Jim (or Jane) we haven't got time for those games' may not only bring the meeting back to the point at issue, but also alert both proponents and respondents to the fact that the former's game has been recognised! Controlling political moves becomes more difficult in the external meeting where members attend as representatives of various organisations. Although the meeting itself may well have a clear purpose, this may not be in accordance with the wishes of any of its individual members. Nevertheless some kind of consensus will be sought. In preparing for this kind of meeting members need to:

1 discover the aim of the meeting

2 discover the attitude and preference of their own organisation. This may have to be presented on a 'sliding scale', running from the ideal preference, through acceptable compromises to an unacceptable position. In such a meeting situation some degree of compromise is almost inevitably required and it will be impossible to satisfy the preferences of all involved

3 discover as much as possible about the other member organisations and their representatives in order to assess their likely preferred positions and fall-back positions. This will require a certain amount of research but such preparation may be well rewarded if only at a personal level. After all, if on meeting another delegate, a member is able to refer to his background, it encourages respect and may start an 'alliance' which can be used later. However in carrying out such research one does need to ensure one gets it right.

CASE STUDY 2.3　　　　　　　　　　　**Unfortunate briefing**

At the Group of Seven summit meeting in Tokyo in July 1993, the USA provided guidance kits to its delegates with the aim of providing details of fellow delegates. Unfortunately the research was somewhat faulty:

- the Italian president, who has no executive power and does not attend such meetings, was shown as leading the delegation, whereas the Italian Prime Minister, who has such power and leads Italy's delegation to the meetings, was not listed;

- details of the other two main members of the Italian delegation, the Treasury and Foreign Ministers, were also omitted, but details of the Finance Minister, who was not due to and did not attend the meeting, were included.

———— KEY TECHNIQUE ————

If information is produced to assist, it must be accurate. If not it is preferable to forget the idea, as faulty information can lose respect, create communication barriers and may even be insulting, albeit unwittingly, thus having the opposite effect to that intended.

Formal meetings

Very often such meetings retain only vestiges of decision making although they may be the ultimate policy control authority. If this is not clearly understood by all members, then the meeting can be hijacked by a member refusing to abide by the generally accepted custom.

CASE STUDY 2.4   **Speak but once**

The ruling Council of one Royal Charter company meets six-monthly in very ornate surroundings, with delegates suitably gowned and operating under very formal rules of procedure. These rules, strictly applied, restrict each member to speaking once only on a subject. When a member did actually speak twice, no one knew how to deal with the situation, whilst to a great extent the question was irrelevant as the 'words were out'. Like the jury told to 'disregard that statement' the audience can hardly oblige.

———— KEY TECHNIQUE ————

The very formality of the meeting and its surroundings can act as a brake on loquacious speakers as the 'speak only once' rule. The difficulty here is that if there are opinions to be put forward, few speakers may wish to speak early in the debate and will attempt to hold back. This tends to encourage alliances between members so that some will act as pace-makers to test the reactions of others leaving the committed members to speak near the end of the debate and to adjust their comments to the arguments already put forward.

Public meetings

Obviously the speaker will need adequate preparation for such an encounter, which will include trying to out-guess his audience so that awkward questions and criticism are established, and more importantly satisfactory answers are framed, in advance. This may enable the force of the question to be dealt with before it is asked. Drawing the sting of the anti-sympathetic delegates will help the speaker attain his aims. Members of the audience wishing to question or criticise the speaker rarely rehearse their comments or practise speaking. Valuable points can be lost simply because the speaker does not know how to put the point across cogently or clearly. Obviously this works to the advantage of the main speaker, although normally he should treat such comments with respect no matter how badly they are presented. Ridiculing a speaker with communication problems may well backfire on the main speaker, particularly with UK audiences who tend to have inherent sympathy with the underdog. Whilst this type of meeting is outside the scope of this book, this point is fundamental and should be appreciated by all seeking to manipulate meetings. Inadequate expertise at presenting arguments and using tactics can lose the game, regardless of the value of the argument.

Rights

The rights of the members at each meeting need to be established and promulgated. Normally all present will have a right or opportunity to speak, but such rights should not, however, be taken for granted. For example, at a meeting of the Board of a limited liability company it will be normal for the Company Secretary to be present. Unlike the members of the Board he or she will not normally have a right to speak, although under current and developing law, there may be an obligation on that person to speak out should the Board or its members be engaged or likely to become engaged in an illegal matter, and so on. Rights should be included in the terms of reference of the meeting.

Networking

The advent of computerisation, and subsequently linking units and systems by electronic processes, has encouraged the use of the option of holding a meeting where participants are remote from one another, yet, by virtue of the technology are still able to communicate. Where a video system is used it is possible not just to communicate by means of printouts and messages on screen, but also for each party to see and hear the other. The advantages are enormous in terms of gaining an instant response with a limited rapport whilst avoiding the costs and strains of travelling, and loss of productive time. Where the terrain is such that travel is impractical, such links can mean the difference between life and death.

CASE STUDY 2.5   **Remote consultation**

In remote Georgia, travel for a medical consultation with a specialist in the state hospital over 100 miles away is very difficult. Local doctors, however, have available a video link which enables them, whilst with their patient, to be linked to a specialist in the hospital and for an in depth consultation to take place.

This consultation can be made even more effective by the use of electronic stethoscopes to magnify the sounds of lungs and heartbeat. X-rays and ultrasound images can also be transmitted, and the latest development would allow the specialist remote from the examination to 'feel' the condition by receiving touch and feel sensations achieved by the local doctor using an electronic glove to examine the patient.

Using such techniques a 'dummy operation' has been conducted with a surgeon operating a robot wielding a scalpel, even though he was over a thousand miles away from the 'patient'.

──────── KEY TECHNIQUE: ────────

It is arguable that a meeting has still taken place even though physically the parties are remote, at least a meeting of minds has taken place.

A further advantage is that the knowledge of the cost of such systems may act as an encouragement to the participants to prepare adequately and to complete their business swiftly. Similarly, if using networking arrangements such as electronic post to transmit requests and information, there is pressure to organise the data into a logical form and to be brief. Many users report feeling a latent pressure to use only the size of the screen for a message which, for those having to deal with parties otherwise inclined to be verbose, may be a welcome relief.

As well as the use within an organisation to pass information between two or more users, thus avoiding the need to meet, systems are being investigated for both smaller and much larger meetings. To try to deal with the interests of 130 000 creditors in over 20 countries throughout the world, Touche Ross, the receivers of the failed Bank of Commerce and Credit International, investigated the concept of holding the meeting via a satellite link. Other companies are considering holding their general meetings via television links with regional centres. At the other end of the scale, it is considered that part of the reason of the rapid growth in homeworking in the United Kingdom has been the easy access to such systems by private individuals. Productivity is considerably enhanced and costs reduced. Although the participants are remote, meetings can take place and business can be transacted.

Drawbacks

The problem with such systems is that they lack one or more of the essential ingredients that are part and parcel of most meetings. Networking links allow for the speedy transmission of information, but communication, since to use the system all messages need to be machine readable, may be slower than would be the case with a telephone conversation or face-to-face meeting. A television link allows both parties to see what is on-screen but not what is just out of the reach of the camera's lens. Above all, what is missing is the social aspect of the work ethic and this must not be discounted when considering the effectiveness of the 'non-physical' meeting. Neither must this aspect of working be ignored when considering how to manipulate meetings. Man is a gregarious creature and even though he may be able to achieve far greater productivity through working without travelling and at hours that suit his body clock, he will miss the interplay with others inherent in the work situation. Further, some people are only able to function when they are in a situation where they relate to others. Whilst some creative people can work best when they are alone, many will claim to be able to garner and foster ideas only by bouncing them off others. This tends to occur in real meetings but may be absent in electronic meetings. A spokesman for a leading UK clearing bank, commenting on the introduction of home-based networking stated, 'this is not to suggest that we shall see a number of companies allowing everyone to stay at home … we are social animals with other colleagues in the workplace'.

Meetings without walls

It should not be overlooked that a meeting held by electronic connection lacks finite boundaries which can have the effect of binding participants together. Using a room for a meeting creates an entity with latent pressure to produce, determine or decide. The very walls themselves act as a latent force, separating the members from the outside world. Networking removes this force and the rapport to the detriment of the meeting.

The social dimension

A considerable amount of business is said to be transacted over meals and on golf courses. Work requires social intercourse and although a number of such relationships, which are forced upon the participants, will be antagonistic, most are not. Most people (94 per cent was the figure quoted in an American study) want to get along with their fellows and are prepared to compromise their own 'best position' in order to attain an acceptable solution. In working with and for other people, we grow to understand them and, even though we may not particularly like them, such propinquity builds relationships which will help progress to be made. In coming together in a meeting it will be easier to reach agreement or a suitable compromise if one knows and understands the other party than if they are a stranger. Language, gestures and body language that emanate from a known colleague are all easier to understand and interpret correctly than those that emanate from a stranger. In contemplating the need to work with people in and out of meetings, getting to know them is perhaps the first requirement. It is for this reason that touring sports teams travel and live closely together, that Boards find they perform better when gathered as an entity in a place remote from the one in which they work, and that a wise supervisor or manager tries to encourage members of the work team to participate in joint activities, and so on. These moves work to create a closer relationship amongst the team to build a rapport and promote better understanding. When those who understand each other come together to discuss problems, there is greater understanding of each other's points of view and a greater chance of agreement. The benefit of this social dimension in terms of gaining agreement and cohesion in meetings is virtually unquantifiable, but extremely valuable and must not be overlooked if we wish to manipulate meetings.

CHAPTER THREE

Face to face

Key learning points

- With one-to-one transactions, a physical meeting is important as eye contact and body language play their part in its conduct

- Adequate preparation and assessment of the other party's possible case may help attain objectives

- Physical surroundings and conditions may affect the outcome and length of the meeting

- Consideration of tactics in advance is essential

The best meeting

It is said that the best committee is a committee of one, since in that way the ideas of the sole participant will normally be swiftly processed by virtue of the total and personal commitment. Similarly, the best meeting may be a meeting of two. Such a meeting satisfies the basic needs of communication outlined previously, that is a two-way flow allowing each party to generate and receive feedback and to check the other's comprehension of the messages being imparted, and to gain further input from the other party immediately. Provided there is consensus, this flow should generate a dual commitment to the decision.

Although the normal understanding of a meeting is of a multi-member gathering, a face-to-face encounter between two participants such as that between A and B referred to in Chapter 1, is every bit as much a meeting as is the 20-person executive meeting held regularly each month. Attempting to set up a one-to-one, face-to-face meeting as an alternative to a more formal one has a great deal to commend it. The aims of both parties may be best assured of success if they actually meet, not just discuss the subject on the telephone. Eye contact and body language are important and cannot be substituted by the telephone, although the advent of videophones may well change this view!

Controlling the encounter

There are other advantages, particularly for the instigator of the one-to-one meeting. Taking the example of A and B meeting in Chapter 1:

1 A, in instigating the meeting, has control of the discussion and the subject matter. He has his aims firmly in view, but must accept that in order to achieve them he must convince B of the value of those views;

2 A, one assumes, having taken the initiative, will be prepared for the encounter and thus has a better chance of manipulating his desired result than B, who is being forced to react without advance planning. In fact, B might be wise to request time to consider the proposal before committing himself;

3 A also has control of the tactics of the meeting and can decide time, place, duration and so on.

Tactics for one-to-one meetings

In waylaying B to ensure the decision is taken rather than deferring it to a multi-member meeting, A can use a number of devices. These devices are set out below.

Promulgating your case

1 Prepare all arguments and facts supporting the case.

2 Consider all possible counter-arguments that B is likely to put forward and prepare defences or counter-arguments.

3 Consider alternatives which, whilst not ideal, may be acceptable to both parties as a fall-back compromise, in order to ensure there is at least a substitutional decision acceptable to both parties.

4 If any loss of face would be involved on B's part, consider ways to avoid this. If face-saving is attempted, that is if there is a concern shown by the instigator to protect the 'reputation' of the opponent, this may help win over the opponent. The recognition by B of this fact may create a rapport.

5 Use devices that apply pressure on B to agree.

6 Guidance of B to make a suggestion which you can then take up as 'B's idea' and agree to, can gain B's commitment. Granting recognition of the other's point of view can be a very effective manipulative tactic.

7 If B's agreement to either the desired result or the substituted result is apparently not forthcoming, a subtle threat of the need to bring the matter up at a meeting might create sufficient pressure to gain agreement.

Creating an acceptance ambience

8 Visiting B in his domain, particularly if senior to him, does not only pay a compliment, but also retains the initiative to the instigator to withdraw should the encounter begin to take too much time.

9 Visiting B in his domain but just before an appointment which you know B must keep, puts pressure on B to agree more swiftly than would otherwise have been the case so that he can free himself from the current meeting to make the appointment.

10 The tactic in (7) above can be extended by A arranging to be 'interrupted' after a pre-set time.

CASE STUDY 3.1 **The unwelcome visitor**

The senior executive had been moved sideways in a management reshuffle and as a result had insufficient work to occupy his day, yet he was a charming individual and an excellent raconteur – 'ideal for a long train journey' as one colleague once

▶

▶ put it 'but just keep him away from my meetings!' The new executive had a considerable workload and although he got on well with the senior and thoroughly enjoyed his reminiscences, he did not have the time available to spend in such chat. Accordingly, he arranged with his secretary that every time the senior visited him, she was to interrupt them with an urgent message or a request for him to return an enquirer's telephone call. An excuse to break off was then provided.

11 Latent pressure is exerted if you remain standing. This exercises a dominance over the encounter and also gives the impression of immediacy – that is 'this shouldn't take too long so I won't bother to sit down'. Both inferences place B under pressure to agree quickly.

12 Arrange to meet on 'neutral ground' but in less than comfortable surroundings so that again pressure is brought to bear on B to agree, particularly if he is a person who likes his creature comforts.

CASE STUDY 3.2   **Espionage**

During a takeover bid, the Director was made aware that bugging devices had been used in the company's offices. He was also being pestered by a number of people who seemed to feel their input was essential. Whilst to a certain extent this was true, the time spent with them was out of all proportion to the information obtained.

--------- KEY TECHNIQUE ---------

Accordingly the Director insisted during a cold January in holding several conversations with such people standing in the middle of the external car park where 'our conversations cannot be overheard'. Somewhat understandably the length of such meetings was swiftly curtailed.

13 If you hold the session in your own office, thus already pressurising B if he is a junior person, and arrange to be 'called away' within a short time of B arriving, discussion can be restricted. A further dimension to this concept can be achieved by holding the session in the Boardroom, or similar 'high-powered' location, and using the 'awe' of the location to affect the more junior person.

CASE STUDY 3.3   **Latent pressure**

The Director was having great difficulty in getting a customer to pay for some products over which there had been a dispute – but more of the 'delay payment' rather than genuine problem type. Knowing the customer had not been to the Head Office, he arranged to meet him there, and, on arrival had him shown into the Boardroom. During the discussion the Director 'took' two telephone calls both concerning debt collection. In both instances the 'conversation' heard by the customer demonstrated the very tough line apparently being taken with dilatory payers including the use of bailiffs. In addition, the Boardroom was an ornate room, beautifully wood panelled and, with concealed lighting and portraits of previous Chairmen, extremely impressive. It gave an impression of solidity and power.

During the subsequent conversation the customer very quickly agreed to pay all but about 5 per cent of the amount outstanding. The cheque was received within two days with a note apologising for the delay and expressing appreciation of the opportunity to view such a 'wonderful room'.

———— KEY TECHNIQUE ————

Care should be taken in utilising this type of approach as the tone, attitude and language need to be adjusted to the encounter. If A was to approach this encounter in too dominating a manner, it could backfire and the respondent might reply as Queen Victoria once said of Gladstone, 'He talks to me like a public meeting'. If this kind of reaction is generated it is unlikely to gain agreement and, indeed, it is more than likely to generate discord.

---

14 If agreement is not forthcoming and it seems that B is resisting all coaxing, a suggestion that the matter be thought over prior to another session at a fixed time on the following day, may create pressure for agreement. In the meantime you may be able to use a third party to promote your cause.

Negotiation

Meetings and their manipulation entail an understanding of the principles of negotiation. In negotiation certain principles must be established and practices observed (*see* Fig. 3.1).

---

1 Establish the facts in order to arrive at an initial view trying to anticipate what will be the other party's view.

2 Accept that there are two sides to every story and that the other party may hold different views (even for apparently illogical reasons).

3 Research the background of the other party and endeavour to assess their likely preferred outcome and manner of approach.

4 Give weight and credence to the views of the other side. Dismissing such views out of hand is likely to provoke a negative backlash as most people want to be recognised and be proud of their contribution. This desire must be appreciated and can be played upon. Well-founded flattery, used with discretion, can be very compelling.

5 Sublimate your own prime preferences to achieve consensus and assess whether there is a substitutional solution acceptable to both. Such 'British compromises' at least have the advantage of allowing things to progress.

6 Try to make constant movements towards the desired result, ensuring that a flexible approach is adopted and that an entrenched position does not close off possible progress towards the ideal or substitutional end.

7 Be ready to compromise, it may not be ideal but at least it may enable progress to be made.

Figure 3.1 Aspects of negotiation

Tactics for face-to-face meetings

In face-to-face meetings a number of tactics can be employed in order to try to ensure one's preferred outcome prevails. These can also be used in meetings where there are more numerous participants but which may become diluted by the increased input. The more notable tactics are set out in Fig. 3.2.

1	Finding the edge.	**9**	Letting the other party make the running.
2	Non-disclosure.	**10**	Silence.
3	Misinformation.	**11**	Rubbing salt in the wound.
4	Face-saving.	**12**	Fishing.
5	Pressure.	**13**	Misunderstanding.
6	Power.	**14**	Playing 'good guy, bad guy'.
7	Threats.	**15**	Temper.
8	Pre-emptive offer.	**16**	Sympathy and under-estimation.

Figure 3.2   Face-to-face meeting tactics

Finding the edge

This involves attempting to discover if there is a fact or any pressure which can be brought to bear on the other party at the meeting. If there is, or it is perceived that there is a hidden agenda (that is, that one of the parties wishes to use the meeting for another purpose or to develop it into something different than that understood at the outset by the other), this may be used against the other player.

CASE STUDY 3.4   **Hidden agendas**

X in Essex and Y in Birmingham were engaged in negotiations usually conducted by post. However Y suggested that they meet in London as he was prepared to travel and could arrange 'other business' which he could deal with at the same time. X agreed to the meeting but with an apparent and considerable show of reluctance. However, what he knew but Y did not know that he knew, was that Y had a girlfriend in London and wanted any excuse to get to the city, particularly if his company would pay his costs of getting there. X then used his apparent reluctance as a lever to exert extra concessions from Y as a *quid pro quo* for re-arranging his diary to oblige Y's with a London meeting.

——— KEY TECHNIQUE ———

Gaining as much information about the other party and their situation and case is essential. Information is power.

Non-disclosure

The principle here is to start the meeting using certain but not all relevant facts. If satisfactory progress towards the object of the encounter is not made, the use at a late stage of additional information or facts may well help the instigator to carry the day. Not using all one's ammunition at the first onslaught does enable a fresh attack to be mounted later. Conversely, sometimes it may be preferable to overwhelm the opposition by means of a pre-emptive move.

CASE STUDY 3.5   **Holding back**

J and K were conducting a rent review discussion. K, as the landlord's agent, was trying to gain the best rent possible and had put forward a number of examples of rents of other nearby shops. J, representing the tenant, had argued the case on the basis of the evidence provided by K. By prolonging the negotiations and using the delay for additional research, J became aware that there was other evidence which would help destroy K's case. However, he did not use this until K had already given way to some extent from the first figure suggested. When J then introduced this additional evidence, K had to further reduce his demand.

——— KEY TECHNIQUE ———

Using the two items separately may contrive advantages greater than using them together.

Misinformation

This involves initially indicating a far worse situation than is really required and then backtracking. Research shows that where this is utilised the hidden (and real) alternative will gain immediate acceptance in over 60 per cent of instances.

CASE STUDY 3.6 **The acceptable price rise**

The manufacturer wished to increase the price of his goods to the customer who would have considerable difficulty sourcing the products elsewhere. Knowing any price increase would be unwelcome, he invited the customer to lunch, thus gaining an edge by playing host. He indicated that prices would have to rise by 10 per cent, and during the sweet and cheese courses, as the customer progressively lost his appetite and argued vehemently against the suggestion, continued to put forward all the facts and evidence for the increase. However, as coffee arrived the manufacturer suggested a compromise 5 per cent increase, which is what he expected in the first place. The customer, relieved that he had avoided a 10 per cent increase, and believing that his vehemence in opposing the suggestion had paid off, readily agreed.

Face-saving

The idea of allowing the other part to save 'face', particularly if the meeting takes place within a high-profile scenario, or on behalf of others, for example negotiating on behalf of trade union members, is a very sound method of manipulating the meeting to agree one's original aim. Since consensus is the desired result, the instigator needs to design the conduct of the meeting to make it appear that both sides have gained something, regardless of the facts – as did the manufacturer in Case Study 3.6 above.

Pressure

Pressure may need to be applied in some meetings in order to achieve progress. Consensus is very acceptable, but often there are differences of opinion, genuinely and sincerely held. Latent pressure may consist of a swift résumé of arguments, perhaps indicating the apparent weakness of the other's case with the aim of gaining agreement, or at least acquiescence as in Case Study 3.3, whereas actual pressure attempts to force the issue. This, however, may put the other party on the defensive and ensure that there is no resolution of the matter.

Power

Inevitably 'pulling rank' exerts pressure simply from the exercise of strength of position. Whilst it can work, like the exercise of pressure, it is risky and may produce a backlash whilst being unlikely to be in the best interests of either party or the business.

CASE STUDY 3.7   **Pulling rank**

The newly appointed divisional Chief Executive had served the Chairman whilst the latter was Chief Executive but had his own ideas on how to operate. At a Board meeting, he put forward such ideas, only to have them ridiculed by the Chairman using the power of his position violently to downtalk the opposition. As a result the Chief Executive completely changed direction and agreed with the Chairman's view.

———— KEY TECHNIQUE ————

In terms of corporate organisation this was a bad development as it was obvious the Chairman still ran the policy of the division. In terms of the Chairman it was bad as he had been allowed to push his own views which were based on an out-of-date understanding of facts and problems; and as far as the new Chief Executive was concerned it was disastrous as he lost face in the eyes of his team. It was also poor in terms of the relationship between Chairman and Chief Executive, as the forceful Chairman was unlikely to respect someone who had abandoned a considered position and crumbled under his onslaught.

Threats

Although in some ways indicating the resolve with which one party views the need to agree business at a meeting, the issue of a threat can only be made once, and although bluff can carry things through, the adage 'never threaten unless you are prepared to carry it out' should not be overlooked. Indeed, since the prime principle of meetings, particularly in one-to-one meetings, is to try to achieve consensus, threats should not really form part of such debate. Having said that, latent threats or hidden power, particularly if the two parties are not on the same managerial level, are present in many encounters.

Pre-emptive offer

One can sympathise with the logic behind this concept. If agreement can be reached on a pre-emptive offer it should certainly cut down on discussion time in the meeting. However, unless the proposal is attractive to the other party, it is risky since it negates the concept of the other party 'justifying their existence'. If the circumstances dictate using a pre-emptive offer, this should be carried out only in conjunction with a face-saver.

Letting the other party make the running

The principle here is to allow the other party to put forward the whole of their case, even including any extra data they were hoping to hold back, before putting forward any arguments or facts oneself. This is one of the principles of interrogation: 'let them say what they want and lead them on'. In other words, whilst someone is speaking he reveals more and more of his case and preferences, allowing the meeting instigator to hold back his ammunition for a final attack.

CASE STUDY 3.8   **Jumped too quickly**

The two sides had been in dispute for some time. Eventually the company decided that it would give way to a limited extent to gain agreement with its supplier. Accordingly, the Director arranged a meeting with his opposite number. Since they had previously reached stalemate one would have thought that as one side had requested a meeting, they had something new to offer. However at the meeting, virtually as soon as it started, the supplier offered to settle at the Director's latest figure.

_____ KEY TECHNIQUE _____

Had they waited to see why the company had requested the meeting they would have found the company had moved towards them, rather than vice versa.

Silence

When Sir Thomas More was facing imprisonment and execution for refusing to acknowledge Henry VIII as head of the church in England he agreed to keep silent on the topic. However the very fact of his silence, in Henry's view, 'screamed up and down throughout Europe'. Silence can indicate a number of attitudes and many people cannot face it. Such people feel a pressure to fill the vacuum by speaking. In speaking, more of their case is revealed, whilst the quiet party gains ammunition for any counter play. Silence is a particularly effective weapon in a two-party, face-to-face encounter but it needs strong nerves to stick with it.

CASE STUDY 3.9   **Steeling one's nerves with silence**

The two agents had agreed to meet, having corresponded for some months, to try to agree terms for a new lease. C, the Landlord's agent, had initially been very bullish, suggesting a high rent but with the remainder of the terms as before. D's arguments on behalf of the tenant had worn him down somewhat and at the meeting, after a re-examination of evidence and counter-evidence a compromise rent was agreed.

C then tried to raise the question of new terms in the lease, at which point D stated that the negotiations had all been on the basis of 'as existing apart from the rent' and that he did not see what more there was to be said. D said the rent had been negotiated and agreed on that basis and that seemed to conclude the discussion. He then kept quiet. C reviewed the situation to where it then rested. D did not reply. C pointed out that the lease was in an old form. D did not reply.

──────── KEY TECHNIQUE ────────

By not replying D put pressure on C, and in the absence of counter-arguments C could only go over old ground again and again – he had nothing left to say.

This resembles the 'punching cotton wool' device, where in answer to a particularly annoyed or outraged other party, if the first party keeps quiet, ultimately the second party runs out of original things to say, keeps repeating themselves and ultimately dries up.

Rubbing salt in the wound

This reactive tactic uses as its conduit the previous activity of the other side. Most people, if they lose out in a negotiation, try to ignore the occurrence thus applying the balm of silence to their wounded pride. However, it may be possible to use the fact that the other side gained the upper hand previously as a lever in the current negotiations.

CASE STUDY 3.10　　　　　　　　　　**The biter gets bitten**

In negotiations over a contract with their American supplier, the UK distributor had been uncharacteristically shafted by the other side, and had been forced to conclude a deal whereby they paid 10 per cent more than they were expecting for goods of a slightly inferior quality.

At the following negotiations, rather than ignoring what had gone before, this fact was referred to again and again, until the supplier caved in and accepted that the previous negotiations had been too one-sided and agreed a deal beneficial to the distribution as part compensation and part apology for the previous tough deal.

Fishing

Keeping quiet forces other parties to speak whereas 'fishing' involves making extreme statements to generate response to keep the other party talking. Again the purpose is to encourage him to disclose more and more of his case, and how deeply he is committed to it.

Misunderstanding

By deliberately misinterpreting the other's comments and statements, the depth of feeling on a particular subject can be revealed. This can also be used in a meeting as a ploy to ruffle the presentation of the person putting forward a case. Conversely, if it is being used against you, you need to be aware of the device and to explain patiently the point again. Indeed, it can be turned against the perpetrator with words such as 'I am sorry you have not understood; I thought I had made it fairly clear but I'll just run through the points again'. If the instigator's aim was to put you off your stroke and draw the meeting to a swift closure, calmly running through the arguments again will be the last thing he wants as it implies inattention or inability on his part.

Playing 'good guy, bad guy'

This is an example of applied psychology, where two partners in dialogue with a third person seem to be at variance with each other. The idea is that a rapport is engendered between the person and the 'good guy' who 'form an alliance' against the 'bad guy'. The aim is then to exploit the rapport thus created in the hope that the person will disclose more of his case or fall back position to his 'friend', the 'sympathetic' listener. Obviously this is more relevant for meetings for three or more persons and brings us into consideration of alliances and ambushes. However the device can be used when the 'bad guy' is not party to the meeting and the 'good guy' attempts to give the impression of forming an alliance with the other person against the 'bad guy' (not present but involved in the subject matter) in order to discover more of the other person's views.

Temper

Deliberate loss of temper during a meeting in order to try to impress the other party how seriously the subject matter is being taken can be effective and act as an indication of commitment. However, it can hardly be re used in the same forum and for this reason should be used with extreme caution.

Sympathy and under-estimation

Trying to engender sympathy for one's present position or problems may engender some rapport but, since it tends to give an impression of weakness, it is unlikely to be successful. Creating in the mind of one's opponent an impression of your own apparent failings, that is an underestimation of ability, may work; however, underestimating one's opponent is a classic mistake, often causing greater disclosure of the case, believing success to be a foregone conclusion.

CHAPTER FOUR

Convening and planning

Key learning points

- Meetings can only be effective if there is considerable planning and forethought

- All those required, but *only* those required, must be present

- Careful attention to aims, composition, agenda, siting, procedure, recording and reviewing the meeting is required to ensure effectiveness

Convening

Assuming all devices for avoiding a multi-member meeting have failed, and there is no alternative, a meeting must be convened. It is essential, if the time to be invested in a meeting is to be well spent, that every effort is made to convene it in a way that encourages the achievement of its purpose(s). There are several items to be taken into account here, but because too often the setting up is regarded as purely an administrative chore, often such aspects fail to gain the attention they deserve and as a result the effectiveness of the meeting is marred.

Aims

If a meeting has no aim it has no reason for existence and should not be held. Its aims are ultimately for the instigator, convener or appointing body to decide. If members go into a meeting not knowing or lacking aims, it is hardly surprising if little comes out. What should come out are decisions. This does not mean that all decisions must be dynamic or entail a change of the *status quo*. After all, if an executive committee meets to review progress towards pre-set aims using criteria already developed, and the data produced for consideration at the meeting shows that, for example, output meets or exceeds those criteria and all the expected progress has been made, no new decisions may need to be made. 'Steady as she goes' may be an apt description for the next stage. Having said that, if all that is required is confirmation that the standards required are being met, the Chairman may be able to avoid the necessity for holding the meeting by confirming that this is the case for all members. Even though, in such a meeting, it may appear that no decision has been made, this is a false illusion, as 'steady as she goes' is nevertheless an instruction and a decision.

CASE STUDY 4.1 **No news is good news – but it still needs to be read**

The committee had been set up specifically to rectify and oversee a number of quality and production difficulties and to ensure former high output levels were regained. Having commissioned and implemented a substantial number of projects, much of the poor performance had been eradicated. At one meeting it was noted that everything was now running in accordance with guidelines and accordingly it was suggested that the committee should not meet the following month as 'there was nothing for it to do'. Despite widespread agreement, one member objected stating that the very fact that it met and it was known to review performance provided a latent control, the lack of which could encourage a reversion to unacceptable standards. The point was accepted, the committee met as usual the following month and was horrified to find a divergence from standards. Had it not met, urgent rectification could have been delayed.

──────── KEY TECHNIQUE ────────

In suggesting there was 'nothing to do' the members overlooked that one underlying aim of the committee was to ensure continued maintenance of the standards.

Inaccurate aims

If a meeting is convened with faulty aims then its achievements are likely to be somewhat haphazard or non-existent, even though it may be possible for benefit to be obtained, albeit by accident rather than design.

CASE STUDY 4.2   **Reference point**

In Case Study 1.2, a meeting was proposed ostensibly so that the new manager could be shown how the system worked. In fact the main reason for the meeting was so that the staff in the Personnel Department could meet and get to know the manager. This was a legitimate aim – but an agenda hidden from the new manager. As far as he was concerned, he spent an hour in the meeting and had to sift from its content the guidance in the operation of the system that he needed and which could have been provided in 30 minutes. The Personnel Department staff certainly gained an impression of him, but it was somewhat faulty as after half an hour he began to grow somewhat impatient at the time it was taking to find out what he wanted to know, which he had mistakenly thought was the purpose of the meeting.

Their impression of him was of a somewhat impatient person, whilst his impression of them was of inefficiency with a marked tendency to waffle. Neither assessment was actually the case, but misinterpretations were the almost inevitable outcome of a meeting convened with faulty aims.

———— KEY TECHNIQUE ————

To avoid this dichotomy, it would have been more effective to have spent, say 10–15 minutes on the Monday outlining the system and to have suggested that they had an informal get together when work was less pressing, or outside working hours, with the sole purpose of enabling them to get to know each other.

Composition

A meeting needs to comprise all those needed to help attain the meeting's aims. However *only* those absolutely required for the progression of business should be present.

CASE STUDY 4.3 **Additional participants additional time**

The Non-executive Director was bemoaning the fact that the Board meetings which used to last four or five hours were now lasting six or seven. 'What else did you expect', replied the Company Secretary, 'you have added four new Board members. If you want them to contribute they must speak. If their contribution is to be valuable in an all day meeting, you must expect them to contribute about 30 minutes each, and thus four of them will add two hours to each meeting.'

———— KEY TECHNIQUE ————

The logic is inescapable, though one would hope that the Chairman, after an initial meeting or two, would be able to drive the meeting forward and keep contributions as short as appropriate. Meetings can lose effectiveness if they last longer than two or three hours.

Basically, if the number of participants is swollen by those who either have no purpose being there or whose contribution is minimal or useless, then effectiveness will be impaired. Restricting membership in this way may need to be qualified with some 'review of business meetings' where the progress of several disciplines is to be considered. Even in this scenario, however, attendance of people not involved in every item may be able to be restricted so that they 'visit' the meeting when required. Obviously this may be difficult to monitor, particularly if, having given their report and left the meeting, a further matter arises affecting their area of responsibility. However this is a situation where the Chairman needs to coach members to prepare for reports from such 'visiting executives' and to try to deal with all matters affecting them during their fleeting 'report only' visits. Alternatively, it may be possible to group disciplines under the control of permanent members of the meeting, and for them each to hold a separate review meeting outside the main meeting to allow non-meeting members the opportunity of reporting in full there. The meeting members can then simply report in outline or on an 'exception basis'. This should mean that the person with 'hands on' responsibility for the discipline may be required only to attend the main meeting on an exception basis.

Timetable

When a meeting is required to be held on a regular basis, the publication of a timetable for such meetings should help both to ensure the attendance of essential members and provide guidance for the preparation and submission of data. Where the attendance of key members is essential for the transaction of business, the duration of the timetable may need to be stretched. Thus, it is not unknown for such timetables to be prepared on a six-month certain, six-month proposed and six-month outline basis and to be firmed up on a rolling six-monthly basis.

Agenda

In using the term agenda, I include both the list of items required to be addressed and the convening of the meeting itself. Most agendas comprise a single sheet of paper and tend to be regarded as of equal value. Its preparation is often given too little attention, being treated as a chore rather than a document that can be used to control and direct the activities of the meeting. Often the merest input is provided to the document, with many originators simply marking up a copy of a previous agenda. Obviously the composition of the agenda must reflect the aims of the meeting and the person responsible needs to consider whether the items put forward do allow this and, if not, whether there is a possibility of generating such data in order to promote the aims.

The preparation of the agenda is reviewed in detail in Chapter 5 but for now it should be noted that it:

- requires considerable attention
- needs to follow a logical and comprehensive format
- needs to be dispatched well in advance of the meeting and
- needs to be accompanied by all the data for consideration at the meeting.

Late data submission

It should be considered entirely unreasonable to table lengthy and complex data at a meeting or immediately before it. In such circumstances it will be virtually impossible for the members to make any reasoned decision or comment on the data, even if accompanied by a summary. The members will then completely be in the control of the originator of the report submitted late, capable of being manipulated by his interpretation of the facts and recommendations. This problem can be compounded by the originator indicating that timing pressures dictate that a swift decision is taken. This immediately counters any suggestion that the matter should be deferred until a following meeting. The whole process is then further complicated by the 'collective decision' concept which will mean that any decision taken will be deemed to have emanated from the whole committee despite, in this case, many members not having been able to read the data on which the decision was based. If something then goes wrong with the project or decision, the perpetrator has the option of sheltering behind such 'collective responsibility', it having been by then conveniently forgotten that his colleagues were required to make a decision without having time to consider the data.

Whilst it may be difficult to avoid falling in with the device the first time round, although abstaining and requesting that a note of the abstention be noted in the minutes is a possibility, it should be made clear that in future a decision will only be forthcoming provided the committee members have had a chance to study the data fully.

CASE STUDY 4.4 **Unable to see the aim for the data**

One of the favourite stories told by Sir Owen Green, former Chairman of the successful and acquisitive UK conglomerate BTR Industries, concerns a man who sold his company to a large combine and became a Non-executive Director. On attending his first Board meeting he was confronted by a high stack of papers for discussion. Immediately he announced that he would not be attending future meetings and swiftly sold his share stake in the combine.

Late tabling of data ensures decisions cannot be properly taken, and can obscure the reality of the situation requiring decisions.

Thinking time

Unlike the orientals who spend a great deal of time considering all aspects of a project or problem before moving into the decision stage, in the western world business decisions are often made with relatively little thinking time. Whichever philosophy is appropriate, and there is something to be said for both, it is difficult to deny that at least some thinking time, if only to consider alternative actions, is essential. After all, although first thoughts, like first impressions, can be very valuable, often further consideration of the business, aided by input from others, may suggest an alternative and preferable route. Requiring a decision without allowing time for thought, original input and data consideration, denies this essential and may be unlikely to lead to good decision making or to the attainment of the aims of the meeting.

Surroundings

The surroundings or location of a meeting can play an important part in determining the type and length of the meeting. If the room is formal and austere then members may be conditioned to make their contributions short and precise, and it is likely that a greater degree of concentration on the subject in hand will be generated. Conversely, if the room is comfortable and relaxed, so too may be the deliberations, and the meeting may lose edge, competitiveness and commercialism.

CASE STUDY 4.5 **Comfort at the price of brevity**

The company had grown rapidly, but the custom of holding Board meetings in the lounge of the founder's house had persisted. However, the fact that members sat in armchairs in a very comfortable lounge almost inevitably led to a more chatty rather than businesslike attitude to the meeting. In addition, the fact that the

▶

▶

owner, the Chairman, was also in fact, if not in intent, playing host, militated against objective consideration of some of his pet plans. Finally, the fact that the Board were meeting in a house rather than an office inevitably led to them taking longer than they would otherwise have taken over the discussion of the business.

──────── KEY TECHNIQUE ────────

The effects on the meeting of its physical surroundings must not be under-estimated. When the meetings were moved to the company's offices the Board lost some of its informality, and meetings lasted half as long. The move also had an effect on the rest of the company which tended to relax when the Board met in the owner's house, as it was five miles distant, but were kept more alert when it met in the office.

If a particular meeting is likely to be contentious then it may be better for it to be held in 'neutral' territory rather than in the home base of one or other of the main protagonists. Using one person's home base, that is their own office, to stage the meeting, gives that person an advantage which can be exploited.

Punctuality

All meetings should start on time. Apart from totally unforeseen or unavoidable delays, if members are allowed to turn up when they like, without agreement or sanction, then the efficiency of the meeting is undermined, apart from it being extremely discourteous to the members who have attended on time. Late arrival can also be used to try to magnify the importance of the latecomer, particularly if such lateness is not challenged by the Chairman. The impression given to those waiting is of disregard – 'what I was working on was more important than any interplay with you'.

To combat tardy timekeeping, no matter who is late, the meeting should start at the time stated and at least deal with some of its formalities, for example, signing of attendance books, approval of minutes, and so on. For this reason, as well as to focus attention on the passing of time generally, the meeting room should contain an accurate clock located in a prominent position. The clock then becomes the independent witness to any lateness. Whilst its presence is useful for combating these ego-games indulged in by some meeting members, for public meetings, for example legally required General Meetings of public listed companies, its accuracy is testimony to the fact that the meeting commenced at the time required.

Finally, in considering punctuality it should not be overlooked that arriving late for a meeting, particularly a one-to-one meeting, may hand the other party an edge.

Time limits

In considering the timing of meetings, setting a time for its conclusion as well as its commencement can help focus attention and train members to be concise in their deliberations. However any such time limit, other than for extreme reasons, must then be strictly adhered to, or the point will be lost. This takes a certain amount of practice, since the Chairman must try to allow sufficient time for the taking of decisions, yet not allow discussion to drag on past the time when a decision could be taken. It is also possible for hijackers to occupy the time of the meeting unnecessarily to ensure either inadequate time is left for consideration of a project they oppose, or to force a decision on a pet topic without sufficient discussion and question. The Chairman may need to use kangaroo, cloture and guillotine measures (*see* Chapter 2) to ensure the meeting adequately concludes its business within the allotted span. If the concept of time limits is new to the meeting, some leeway may be necessary in the first few meetings under such a regime.

Protection

Assuming that the meeting has legitimate purpose and effective aims, time is needed to determine decisions. However decisions themselves require concentration – a process which needs to be protected. Concentration is destroyed by interruptions and these must therefore be countered or minimalised, since even a very tactful and quiet intrusion to pass a message to a member can destroy the rapport and concentration. The focusing of thought on the subject matter is broken since the interruption, be it the telephone or a personally delivered message, is a reminder of the outside world and other matters. In addition, since movement attracts attention, a person coming into the room automatically draws the eyes, breaking concentration. All interruptions, except in the direst emergency, and particularly any which are deliberately staged to enhance the prestige of the target, should be outlawed.

Procedure

Although the level of formality of the meeting will differ widely according to custom, it is usual for the minutes of the previous meeting to be confirmed and for all members to sign a book of attendance or for their attendance to be noted in some way. This can assume an importance out of all proportion to its apparent bureau-cratic overtones. If minutes of the previous meeting are approved at the next meeting by those attending the previous meeting, and are then signed as evidence of the transactions at that previous meeting, then they stand as prima facie evidence of what transpired. The minutes can be challenged but this challenge may be difficult to sustain when a signed copy is available evidencing such agreement to their accuracy.

CASE STUDY 4.6   **Not guilty**

The company failed and was subjected to an investigation. It seemed that certain irregularities had been perpetrated and action was being considered against the Directors. The Non-executive Directors were extremely concerned at the irregular-ities that had been uncovered. After investigation they pointed out that, as disclosed by the signed copies of the minutes of the various meetings that they had attended, information regarding the irregularities had not been given to the Board, such details only having been made known to some of the Executive Directors.

———— KEY TECHNIQUE ————

Preparing and gaining approval of minutes as evidence of what took place and what was decided, preserves a document of record for later reference.

Speaking and voting

Generally members at a meeting should address and speak through the Chairman. This may, however, lead to a level of formality inappropriate to the occasion and in many cases is considerably relaxed, particularly to allow in-depth consideration of certain business, for example strategy reports and so on, where opinions, estimations and judgements, rather than facts, may be required. At times however, the formality can be required to be maintained at a level out of all proportion to the situation.

CASE STUDY 4.7   **Formal to a fault**

At the first meeting of the Governors of a primary school after the election of parent representatives, the Chairman turned to one of the new members and said 'Mrs Smith, would you wish to address the body of the meeting, through the Chair, on matters of interest to you'.

The level of formality of language used was out of all proportion to the occasion and to the members present and had the effect of ensuring that the new members hardly said a word. A more friendly, 'Jo, we congratulate you on your election and welcome you to your first meeting as a Governor. Is there anything you wish to say?' would have been more appropriate.

--------- KEY TECHNIQUE ---------

Of course it is always possible that the Chairman had a hidden agenda, in this case the stifling of parent comment from the outset.

Usually, particularly with a meeting which has been in being for some time where the members know each other and each other's views well, there should seldom be any need for a formal vote. In most cases business is agreed by consensus. However, if and when a formal vote needs to be taken, individual member's voting power needs to be understood clearly and may need to be checked against the terms of reference or appointment. This is particularly relevant as far as the voting power of the Chairman is concerned, in order to establish whether he has a second or casting vote available to ensure any deadlock is broken. Having said that of course, if a casting vote is needed it is indicative that half the members are not in favour of the item which hardly bodes well for its successful introduction.

Gaining the sense of the meeting

In board meetings, as well as in many other types of meeting, decisions reflect the 'collective responsibility' concept and the Chairman should summarise the arguments before taking the 'sense' or decision of the meeting. In most meetings each person entitled to be present has a right to be heard on each subject and this will usually be the case in most other meetings, as any alternative negates the purpose of the member's attendance. Whilst with a committee of long standing the Chairman may be able to gain the sense of the meeting by means of a fairly informal question such as 'anyone anything else to say?', with a newer committee or meeting, a more structured approach may be necessary. To generate an individual contribution the Chairman might wish to address a member by name 'Ted, I think you wished to contribute to this discussion but I don't recall hearing from you, do you have anything to add?' Even if Ted has nothing to add, he may well say a few words and will feel flattered that his contribution has been sought. If there has been some dissent or argument, the Chairman might wish to try to gather the threads together by addressing the leaders of disputing factions with such words as: 'Mary, are you sure you have now put all the facts to the meeting?' or 'Bill, have you had enough time to put your case?' Assuming both do contribute they will normally try to gain support from any waverers by summarising their most salient points. From their comments the Chairman can check that he has all the facts needed to provide an overall summary. Using this approach it should be difficult for anyone to complain of unfair treatment.

CHAPTER FIVE

Controlling the agenda

Key learning points

- Manipulation can only take place after adequate preparation

- Meeting members need instant command over salient, and reliable, information

- Manipulation can be effected by late submission of data and countered by stipulating adherence to data submission rules

- Meetings can be controlled by devising a guide to content, submission, and formulation of agenda

Preparation

Despite meetings being very different in content and style, all members should prepare adequately. Meeting organisers should be able to assume that members will prepare and have information and data, at least for that area for which they are responsible, readily to hand or memorised. Assumptions can be dangerous however and in this connection the adage that 'assume' makes an 'ass' of 'u' and 'me' could not be more apt. Repeatedly one experiences situations in which members attending a meeting have failed to prepare and lack essential data.

This is not simply a question of being able to fight, or defend, one's own corner, or to make one's own case. If it were that would infer that one only attends a meeting in order to report on one's own area of responsibility. Whilst there may be meetings requiring that type of limited input, most meetings are constructed to take collective decisions. As far as boards of directors of limited companies are concerned, for example, this doctrine of collective responsibility is virtually enshrined in law, whilst moves from the European Community would make each director personally liable, unless he could prove his own blamelessness, for the actions of every other director. In such circumstances, members do not need to prepare solely for their own report, but to have information and views on all subjects on the agenda. Many people being promoted from manager to director fail to understand the need to relegate the interests of one's own discipline to the overriding interests of the organisation as a whole, and to prepare accordingly.

CASE STUDY 5.1　　　　　　　　　　**Challenging truth economy**

The Director attending the Board prided himself on having an excellent memory, particularly for figures, and was thus somewhat puzzled when he realised that figures being quoted by one of his colleagues were at variance to his recollection of such figures. When this occurred for the third or fourth time, he became intrigued and took the trouble to check the figures now being asserted as the comparables. He found that his recollection was accurate and the figures being put forward were incorrect. So that he could challenge this when it recurred, he started an analysis sheet on which, for each monthly report, he could record the salient statistics.

──────── KEY TECHNIQUE ────────

This statistics sheet became a valuable record in its own right and once it was known that it was available, few committee members tried to repeat the device of using false figures, or 'accidentally' misquoting figures.

Fact control

If one is to try to make a point, or convert the meeting's views to accord with one's own, then it is essential to have complete command over all the relevant facts and figures so that challenges cannot be mounted. Not having information and data to hand can destroy your case in the eyes of the meeting and will destroy any control of the situation you are trying to convey. Unfortunately computerisation has led to a proliferation of information which can bombard and threaten to engulf organisations and all those who work within them. Much of what is available is non-essential or even irrelevant and time needs to be devoted to identifying and assimilating the essential, whilst discarding the rest. The Director in Case Study 5.1 realised that preparing his own 'salient features' analysis was preferable to trying to refer, during a meeting, to the complex management information package that was produced for each of four operating divisions. Soon other members came to rely on his research for speed of access and accuracy and it was realised that the group management would benefit if each reporting package contained a similar 'instant access' summary.

Making the case

Confidence in the perpetrator of business in a meeting can be a valuable part of gaining support, which is where administrative back-up, in terms of preparation and command of data and information, is essential. Even then sometimes luck plays a part.

CASE STUDY 5.2   **Lady Luck to the rescue**

Without notice, and given limited time, the Director had been forced to estimate the cost of fitting out new premises acquired late the previous year and now, early the following year, had to apply to the Board for additional funding as that estimate had been totally understated. Ignoring the fact that the timetable under which they had requested him to provide the original estimate was totally unrealistic, the Board were extremely critical of the cost excess. The Director pointed out that much of the additional cost was due to increased fire precaution materials. 'But why wasn't this costed in last December?' was the retort. 'It was in part, but it now reflects new and additional requirements', was his instinctive response. In this way

▶

▶

he deflected the criticism, believing that no one would check whether additional fire precaution requirements had actually been brought into force. He was somewhat nonplussed to later discover that his 'explanation' was actually completely accurate and such requirements had indeed been implemented.

———— KEY TECHNIQUE ————

In fact, having been ambushed, it could be said that he fought the wrong battle. Rather than instinctively reacting to and deflecting criticism with what he hoped was an uncheckable story, he should have carried the battle to the enemy and pointed out that if you ask for an estimate for fitting out a 100 000 sq ft building in 48 hours between Christmas and New Year, thus allowing totally insufficient time for detailed estimates, checking planning requirements and measurements, and obtaining clearance from the Fire Officer, it is hardly surprising if such estimates are incorrect

Determining the data

A study of the agenda should help determine both the data required for the Board, and the scope of such data. As far as the Chairman and the Secretary are concerned, their responsibility is to ensure that an agenda is developed that moves the meeting towards its aims, calls for the submission of information (and all the information) that will satisfy this requirement and generates the supply of such information to all those required to contribute to the making of the necessary decisions. The framing of the agenda places considerable power in the hands of its originator, since if an item is omitted it may be difficult to find time for it to be considered on the day, and thus a decision which one member might have wanted may have to be postponed. The order of items on an agenda is usually indicative of value and support, and positioning an item in a low position can imply a lack of importance, and, if time limits are applied, that it may not be reached before the meeting runs out of time.

Conversely, some organisations prefer to deal with routine matters first in order to 'clear the decks' before proceeding to deal with special or strategic issues, particularly where the amount of time to be spent on such matters may be elastic. In this instance placing an item high up the agenda may indicate relatively low importance, but at least it should ensure it gets a hearing.

Aims of a meeting

The positive advantages of meetings having aims have already been mentioned. This can be summed up in the phrase, 'unless I know what the target is, how do you expect me to take aim'. Whilst such aims may be couched in fairly general terms for a series of meetings, the aims of individual meetings can be made far more specific. In both cases they can act as a directive force on the meeting, creating a pressure on the meeting members to achieve. Although a Board of Directors might have as the aims of their regular meetings:

- maximise profit to at least £X million in the current financial year without using additional capital;
- keep employment costs to not more than 25 per cent of gross margin;
- earn Y per cent return on capital employed;
- achieve output of 105 per cent of previous financial period;
- maintain quality and service, to levels as defined.

And so on. These are outline statistical guidelines or strategies, within which it is possible to adopt a number of alternative actions or tactics. The horizon and timetable of action of the Board is essentially long-term and as long as the meeting ultimately achieves the aims, there may be deviations in the short-term from such criteria. The fact that the Board has such long-term aims does not mean it cannot also have short-term aims, related to specific problems and/or projects. Reflecting the aims, or a synopsis, at the start of the agenda is a reminder to all members of priorities.

The dynamic agenda

Single or *ad hoc* meetings can, of course, have far more specific aims, to which many members may find it easier to relate. Being specific, the aims create more pressure on the meeting members to deliver. The Chairman wishing to control and direct the meeting may find that incorporating such aims in the notice helps to focus the attention of the members on the required outcome. For example, if he needs to reduce staff

---

AGENDA

for an informal executive meeting to be held on
[date one week ahead]
in the Company Boardroom at 2 pm prompt
Subject: Absenteeism

Aims of meeting: To devise and implement up to five tactics or initiatives for immediate implementation to reduce absenteeism to near or below the industry average.

Items for discussion:

1 To consider monthly reports of staff absenteeism over past 12 months. (See brief résumé attached.)
2 To compare such reports with analyses of absenteeism throughout the industry. (See report from [Industry] Trade Association attached.)
3 To consider whether there are special reasons for this company's poor performance, and if so what can be changed/improved to ensure a reduction.
4 To determine five or more methods to ensure such a reduction. Members will be expected to attend with ideas for consideration at the meeting, such ideas must be capable of implementation within 14 days.

Administration: The meeting duration will be 2 hours.
No interruptions or messages.

Attendance: Personnel Manager, Company Nurse, Company Secretary, Works Manager, Sales Manager.

Notes:

a) Setting the meeting a week ahead should allow ample thinking time.

b) Providing internal statistics with external comparisons sets the problem in context with the delay before the meeting, allowing time for assimilation of the data.

c) Requesting members' ideas ensures accountability.

d) Stating that there must be no interruptions not only allows meeting members to brief their staff but also underlines the importance attached to the subject by the Chairman. It is not unknown for some meeting attendees to arrange for deliberate interruptions to meetings either to enable them to escape some agenda items or simply to try to bolster their own importance.

e) The tone and structure of the agenda itself seeks to demonstrate that action is required. It implies an urgency since the subject needs urgent rectification.

Figure 5.1   Draft dynamic agenda

absenteeism, he might convene a meeting of the heads of Personnel, Legal, Accounting and the appropriate representative of the largest department, and stipulate in the agenda that the aim is to develop five suggestions that will reduce absenteeism from its current unacceptable level to a pre-stated target. On receipt the meeting members should commence a consideration of the problem so that their in-meeting deliberations are a secondary, rather than primary, response. The meeting will also benefit by having already given members valuable thinking time.

Agendas should not be used simply as a static list of topics for discussion. They can and should be dynamic, as this will:

- focus attention
- engender action
- act as a reminder and
- prompt the preparation, collation and submission of data.

If, instead of issuing a dynamic agenda as set out in Fig. 5.1, the Chief Executive had said, 'I think we need to get together to consider absenteeism', the aim is woolly, and the manner of convening the meeting is haphazard. Both provide signals – neither of which is indicative of sound preparation or control – to those involved. A request couched in those terms is likely to generate a pretty woolly and inconclusive discussion.

Reviewing the content

The composition of the agenda should be reviewed periodically to ensure that the most effective format is being used and that all business regarded as regular is still required.

CASE STUDY 5.3   **Redundant**

The Secretary had noticed that one regular item on the agenda which he had inherited from his predecessor seemed to pass the members of the meeting 'on the nod'. One month by mistake it was omitted, and as a result did not appear for four or five months. Eventually its omission was noted, but it was agreed that the information had outlived its usefulness and could be removed officially from the business of the meeting.

There can be a temptation to make 'a mistake' and to remove apparently pointless items from agendas for regular meetings. This is dangerous, since often the information may be required for the 'steady as she goes' type of decision, rather than to initiate change. There should be an inviolable rule that no item can be removed from the agenda of a regular series of meetings without the agreement of the meeting itself and/or of the Chairman.

The composition of an agenda will inevitably depend on the type of meeting being convened; however, examples of the possible sources of such items are set out in Fig. 5.2.

---

1 **The timetable of business.** Required to be considered by the meeting with regular business supplemented by one-off or time/occasion generated business.

2 **Items from an earlier meeting.** Most meetings will, on occasion, need to leave over some business for later or further consideration. This is not simply a question of repeating the agenda item but of examining the reason for the postponement of the decision and, should this be to await fresh data, checking whether this is now available and, if so, ensuring it accompanies the agenda or is otherwise submitted in good time for the meeting.

3 **New business.** The incorporation of new business on the agenda will normally need the Chairman's prior approval. After all, if the aims of the meeting have been set, only new business, which enables those aims to be met or worked towards, should be included. In this way the attention of the meeting is focused exactly on those matters for which it was set up. Again the Chairman's power of being able to determine what business the meeting may discuss can be considerable.

4 **Items requested by members.** These may require the Chairman's prior approval for similar reasons to those noted under 'new business'.

5 **Regular control reports.** The point has already been made that checks for effectiveness and continued requirement should be made of such data to avoid cluttering the meeting with consideration of information no longer having real significance.

6 **Market, economic, legal or other changes.** Considerable care needs to be taken to check that such data is entirely relevant to the aims of the meeting before incorporating it. Nevertheless meetings do need to avoid becoming introverted and to ensure that they are ready to react to changing circumstances.

Figure 5.2   Meeting business sources

7 Statutory or similar required items. For example, for a company Board the agenda would need to contain at certain times, approval of Directors' report, dividend recommendations, and so on.

Notes

a) These sources are provided for example only and are not meant to be exhaustive.

b) Grouping like items will aid the flow of the meeting.

c) Following a set format will also assist the flow of the meeting.

d) As an inviolable rule the agenda should be dispatched at least seven days prior to the meeting with all the data required for members' consideration.

Figure 5.2   Continued

Accompanying data

Many items will require data to be distributed to each member and sufficient time must be given for its study. This means that guidelines for such preparation and submission may need to be issued.

CASE STUDY 5.4   **Impossible task**

The trustees of a pension fund met regularly each quarter. Over the years the custom had developed at the meeting of tabling the minutes of the previous meeting, accounts and detailed investment reports. A new trustee, lacking the benefit of the other members' familiarity with the subject and the reports, complained, with considerable justification, that it was impossible for him to make any reasoned comment or judgement on the content of the reports and thus to justify his presence or to perform the duties entrusted to him by the members.

——— KEY TECHNIQUE ———

Issuing data in this way may seem to some to be an effective way of manipulating meeting members as they may be forced to make decisions based on insufficient consideration of, or knowledge of, the subject matter. Whilst this may be necessary and acceptable on occasion, constant use of the device negates the purpose of the meeting since effectively it reduces the meeting to the status of a 'rubber stamp', having to agree actions already virtually taken. It was of course a variation of such an approach that enabled Robert Maxwell to divert to his own ends so much money from the pension funds under his control.

Ensuring meeting effectiveness

If guidance such as that set out in Fig. 5.3 is issued, members will be put on notice as to what is required of them and cannot then complain of the unexpectedness of a request for data. It is also a sound way of creating habits.

Requirements to be issued to all meeting members and those submitting information to be considered at the meeting.

A. Timetable

1 A timetable for the use of all required to attend, submit data to, and draw information from the meeting will be prepared on a rolling six-month basis and will be issued by the meeting convener.

2 Other than in the most exceptional instances, the timing of meetings will not be changed and any member unable to attend must let the meeting convener know as soon as possible.

3 An agenda with supporting data should always be issued at least seven days prior to a meeting.

B. Data required

1 As a matter of routine all information and reports should be made available to the meeting convener eight working days before the meeting.

2 All data should be submitted with the stated number of copies required. The stated number should be the number of persons entitled to receive the agenda plus any required to be sent out for information, plus, say, one spare for each of the five persons on the distribution list. *Note:* Where it is usual for a number of documents to accompany the agenda, colour coding such documentation could be considered.

Figure 5.3   Requirements for data submission for meeting

3 If data is not available to meet the submission deadline an indication of the availability date must be given. The Chairman must be informed and a note of the expected date of receipt/issue must be entered on the agenda.

Note: Those submitting data late must make every effort to convey it direct to the meeting members prior to the meeting with the required number of spares to the meeting convener. Asking for data to be allowed to be tabled at the meeting, particularly if it consists of detailed, involved or lengthy reports may result in the item being 'left on the table' for consideration at a later meeting.

4 Documentation will be presented in agenda order

C. Presentation

1 Every item prepared for the [Board/committee] will need a standard covering sheet (see later).

2 Subsequent sheets may be presented in the format most suitable for the subject matter.

3 The utmost brevity, commensurate with the subject matter, should be employed. Commentary should be avoided and facts and suppositions, and opposing data, suitably differentiated, must be presented clearly.

4 Source(s) of data should be referenced and a summary used, rather than including such data as part of the submission.

5 The conclusions and recommendations, as required to be set out on page 1, must be clearly evidenced within the report.

6 Plain English should be used and jargon avoided. Where jargon is essential, a glossary which accurately defines the terms used should be included.

D. Supporting commentary

1 At the meeting, the report's originator or person responsible for the subject matter should be prepared to speak about the report, to answer questions from other members and generally to assist the meeting to come to a suitable decision regarding its content.

2 Should the meeting require amplifying documentation this must be provided in the same format as that used in the original report and submitted for the following meeting.

3 Proposers should endeavour to speak only once to support or promote the subject matter and should therefore cover all salient facts in their short presentation.

Note: This will entail marshalling all facts, data, comments and so on, balancing brevity against comprehensiveness, highlighting only the most important aspects and avoiding repetition, other than when necessary as a result of other members' questions.

4 Other meeting members should similarly endeavour to speak only once, putting forward their objections or comments in the same manner as set out in D3 above.

Figure 5.3   Continued

5 After such proposals and counter-comments, if the subject is of such import, the Chairman may wish to encourage a short general discussion on the subject, otherwise the next move will be to summarise the content and take the sense of the meeting.

E. Decisions

Decisions will be communicated by the meeting convener and/or the sponsoring member. If approved or referred back for reconsideration the decision will be supported by a copy of the minutes dealing with the subject which will include any conditions, timing, capital expenditure, and so on.

Organisation name

Report title...Date of report..

Author/sponsoring dept...

Date to be considered by meeting...

Subject matter...

Recommendations 1 ....

               2 ....

               3 ....

Résumé of facts/contentions supporting recommendations ....

....

....

....

Résumé of facts/contentions contesting recommendations..

....

....

....

Figure 5.3   Continued

Implications for organisation if not proceeded with...

....

....

....

Capital expenditure implications...

....

Skill/personnel implications...

....

Timing required..

An outline required on first page of all board/committee reports

Note: Formal rules of debate may be applied in certain circumstances and/or organisations. The following is a résumé:

1 In order for business to proceed it will be expected that business will receive support from at least one other member of the meeting who will normally second the proposal.

2 If no support is forthcoming then the Chairman will have authority to rule that no further discussion will ensue and the proposed item will fail.

3 The proposer of an item of business, having put the business to the meeting, will have a right of reply to points raised against it by other members.

4 Normally each member, other than the proposer, will be able to speak on each item of business once only.

5 Once business has been put to the meeting, other than with the consent of the meeting, it cannot be withdrawn.

Figure 5.3   Continued

CHAPTER SIX

The Chairman and the Secretary

Key learning points

- Good chairmanship, with clear aims, drive and personality, is essential to the success of the meeting

- The power of the Chairman is considerable and needs to be used positively to achieve the meeting's aims

- Assessing members' preferences and aversions in advance may help the Chairman achieve these aims

- A Secretary's input in providing low-key but efficient administration, and preparing an objective record of what transpired is also essential

Two key players

Whilst every meeting is different and every requirement varies, there are two key players common to most meetings – a Chairman and a Secretary. The titles may differ but someone must lead the discussion and someone else should take notes of decisions. Effective meetings need both and as key players their joint and separate impact on the meeting can be considerable. The Chairman normally needs to have a high-profile, even extrovert, approach, whereas the normal role for the Secretary is far more low key.

The quintessential manipulator

The position of the Chairman is pivotal in terms of the effectiveness of the meeting and its approach to and determination of its work, and how such work and the members are manipulated and guided. Whether the meeting be that of a Board running a company or a hospital, a committee running a factory or a garden fête or an action group campaigning against an unpopular proposal or decision, the meeting itself will normally reflect far more the character, drive and inspiration of the Chairman than any other factor or member. If this is not so then it is likely that the meeting is being dominated by someone other than the Chairman which may not be ideal.

Whilst having separate responsibilities, there needs to be considerable interface between the Chairman and the Secretary to ensure efficient and effective meetings. Both must be aware of their duties and responsibilities. The Chairman needs to undertake all the items set out in Fig. 6.1.

---

1   To take responsibility for pushing the meeting itself to consider all its business, but only its business, and to attain its aims.

2   To be conscious of what is trying to be achieved from each item of business and from the entire meeting.

3   To ensure that not only is each item on the agenda dealt with comprehensively, but also that all members are heard on the subject, which may mean actively inviting members to contribute, rather than passively waiting for them to do so.

4   To bring the meeting back to the business in hand should it stray from such considerations.

5   To close down members' arguments or contentions where these threaten to swamp consideration of the subject matter and are not progressing the discussion. This is particularly relevant if the meeting is subject to a time limit. The problem is that often the value of such members' contributions is in inverse proportion to the amount of time they spend propounding it. Moving the meeting on can then take a great deal of tact.

6   To ensure that the decisions arrived at are recorded and promulgated and that subsequent meetings are arranged only when business requires.

7   To lead the discussion and the meeting itself. A Chairman is a leader and an effective leader is someone who makes things happen and achieves results through people. The required work of a Chairman is thus to seek to make things happen through the members.

Figure 6.1   Responsibilities of the chairman

Positive power play

The purpose of the meeting may have been established before the appointment of the Chairman but regardless of this there is no doubt that he will both affect and interpret those aims in his own way. The meeting will be 'his' meeting in the same way that companies with high-profile chairmen are regarded almost as being in their ownership and are certainly in their control. After all, the Chairman in that context is usually the highest power within the organisation and very often what he prefers becomes policy or practice. This gives the Chairman a great deal of power which must be used carefully and with discretion but can, of course, also be used less responsibly to attain personal aims.

The Chairman will know the purpose of the meeting, and by virtue of his position must endorse that purpose, so will wish to see the items of business considered by the meeting moved towards the attainment of the purposes. If he becomes aware of any possibility of this aim being frustrated, he may feel it to be his responsibility to try to 'take out' or 'neutralise' the opposition. Since this may be difficult in the meeting itself, as it will gain attention and the opposition might gain support, it may be best for him to take the initiative in advance of the meeting.

CASE STUDY 6.1   **Checkmate**

The insurance company had asked for a meeting with the pension trustees to discuss various matters. The Chairman suspected that part of the reason for them requiring the meeting was to raise the question of increasing the fees paid for additional administration work carried out. Accordingly, before the meeting took place he made it known to the brokers for the fund, who would also be attending the meeting and who interfaced regularly with the insurers, that he wished to consider the performance of the insurers over a long period and hinted at a possible change of insurer. The matter of increased fees was not raised.

——— KEY TECHNIQUE ———

Knowledge or even anticipation of the possibility of the other party's agenda can help meeting members out-manoeuvre the opposition.

CASE STUDY 6.2   **Constructive diversion**

The Chairman became aware that a Board member intended raising the question of standards of on-site safety at the Board. He was also aware that the Director responsible was under great pressure and were such an emotive matter to be raised in a public forum, an argument was certain to develop. Accordingly, he set up an informal discussion before the Board to consider how safety standards could be improved. In such a neutral atmosphere and under duress from the Chairman, a joint approach using the skills of both parties in harmony was developed. The Board simply received a brief verbal report of the initiative.

——— KEY TECHNIQUE ———

Once again knowledge is seen to be power. In this instance the Chairman was made aware of the development by the Secretary who acted as his confidante and shop floor 'ears and eyes'. As an alternative the Chairman needs a high-profile presence so that he becomes aware personally of the developments, or has sufficient perception to second guess them.

Carrying the meeting along

Chairmanship relies a great deal on personality, and a strong personality, to carry both business and members along, in order to manipulate the meeting so that its aims are achieved. The Chairman needs to have:

- vision, to move the meeting towards the attainment of aims
- good communication skills so that his vision is easily communicated to the other meeting members
- enthusiasm to motivate members so that they learn to believe in plans and in their own ability to perform and achieve them
- the ability to delegate, to force decision making and accountability down the chain

of command, not so that someone at a low level is left 'carrying the can', but to widen their horizons, make them aware of the issues and encourage them to make suggestions.

CASE STUDY 6.3 **Laying on the line**

The Chairman in his opening address to the new divisional Board, not only welcomed all members but stated that the Board would be run as informally as possible, but that this would be matched by a need for total accountability and commitment. He added that he only wanted members at the meeting who were prepared to operate under those guidelines and invited anyone not prepared to do so to leave the meeting. No one moved.

——— KEY TECHNIQUE ———

This public declaration acted as considerable peer pressure on all present.

The four aspects of good chairmanship set out above need to be exerted at all times during a meeting in order to gain consensus among the members and to move the meeting. In doing this the Chairman is essentially manipulating the members as well as the meeting itself.

Controlling the members

In fact this may not be difficult since if people can identify with a successful effort they tend to co-operate and work more effectively. If they have something of which they can be proud, and know that their contribution is important to the meeting and the organisation, they tend to commit to a far greater degree than is otherwise the case. In any event basic involvement tends to create an environment where individuals work willingly.

Each of these aspects of controlling the members infers that the Chairman will motivate the members, for example, by the judicious use of praise, and by allowing them to bring to the meeting certain problems for discussion and assistance. Even though such business may be outside the strict aims of the meeting, allowing such discussion will allow them to be shared. This should engender a positive attitude.

Within an established meeting consensus may often be achieved, although there may be instances when conflict will surface. Indeed it is arguable that a certain amount of constructive conflict can generate ideas and move the meeting towards its aims. If destructive conflict arises, the Chairman needs to be able to either remove it or direct it positively. If, for example, he is aware that A is not in accord with B on a particular issue, he will need to highlight aspects of the subject matter where they are in agreement, before moving on to areas of disagreement with the benefit of some unanimity.

CASE STUDY 6.4   **Impasse**

The Board were at a complete impasse. Trade was poor and the financial situation of the company was critical. The Chairman felt that the reaction to that scenario was to 'trade out of the problem' by investing more money in people and promotion. Other Directors felt that this was totally wrong and every effort should be made to cut costs in order to survive. These two opposing viewpoints were reconciled by the Secretary suggesting that the real problem was that losses were being incurred and that that was the real priority to be faced. Having got some unanimity there, the Board then developed a step-by-step approach, based on twin concepts of time and cash flow.

———— KEY TECHNIQUE ————

Reconciling differences may be impossible, but cementing agreements on items where there is agreement can act as a foundation for further progress.

Motivating members

The role of Chairman combines that of 'first among equals' with that of leader and this dual role should always be recognised. In the latter endeavour the Chairman should ensure the best of each member is brought out within the meeting. It can be easy for a dominant person to take over the meeting and for less dominant members to be overshadowed to such an extent that they make little or no contribution. If this occurs then the Chairman's responsibility is to encourage the quieter members to make a contribution, even, if necessary, silencing others in order to for them to do so. In this the Chairman will need to adopt the guidelines set out in Fig. 6.2.

---

1 Ensure that everyone knows why they are present. In this the Chairman may need to restate the meeting's objectives. He may also state the time within which he would like to see the business conducted. Such strictures must be promoted positively, the aim being to complete the business properly, recognising that time is scarce and valuable.

2 Treat every member as an individual with rights to make the points he or she wishes. This may require the Chairman actually to invite a contribution by name from the 'less forward' members.

3 Encourage every member to identify with the body as a whole and to relate to every other member. This will take time and, with some members, can be difficult.

4 Encourage a sense of pride in the meeting and its achievements. Without being excessive, the Chairman should praise achievements whether these be joint or individual. As a nation we in the United Kingdom tend to criticise too much and praise too little, even though praise (which costs nothing) can be the most powerful motivator and incentive. It is also helpful when trying to manipulate a meeting since this 'feel good' effect can stifle or neutralise what could otherwise be objections.

5 Ensure that all members are treated fairly and given a chance both to explain their views and attitudes and to argue their case. Obviously this in turn requires the opposition to have a chance to do the same. If members see that each is allowed his own turn to put forward arguments, the temptation to filibuster or use other means by which the arguments of others are not heard should be reduced.

6 Ensure that members feel that business which they feel is important does get discussed. This may be difficult in the early life of a meeting and the Chairman needs to be tactful in accepting or rejecting business requested by members. If it is entirely germane to the business in hand, it may be worth considering, even if that in turn means the meeting overruns its allotted time span. If it is not appropriate, a tactful suggestion 'perhaps we could have an initial chat about that after the meeting' might solve the problem without disincentivising the member.

Figure 6.2   Motivating the meeting

Negative power play

Whilst most aspects of the checklist in Fig. 6.2 require positive power play in order to achieve the aims of the Chairman, which will normally be closely identified with the aims of the meeting itself, there may be times when the Chairman will indulge in negative power play in order to promote his own pet theory or practice. Company directors are supposed to act in a fiduciary capacity and in the best interests of the company, meaning that they act as trustees for the owners or shareholders, and should not be in a position where their own interests conflict with those of the company. This fiduciary aspect may not be required of members of other meetings, but nevertheless members need to be careful that the Chairman, who has considerable power over the meeting, does not abuse his position in this way.

Negative power play can be effected by the Chairman:

- stressing and representing with approval and bias arguments put forward
- suppressing aspects of arguments which do not support his preferred action and
- slanting the summing up of the discussion before taking the sense of the meeting.

CASE STUDY 6.5   **Lose your temper – lose the argument!**

The Divisional Director was concerned that policies originated by the Chairman, but now somewhat outdated, were holding back the performance of the division. He prevailed upon other members of the Divisional Board to support him in attempting to get alternative policies at least tried on an experimental basis. However, when this was raised at the Board and gained some support, the Chairman lost his temper and told the members to continue to implement the tried and tested procedures rather than 'wasting time on new ideas'.

———— KEY TECHNIQUE ————

Whilst the Chairman might have been right, it would have been more constructive to have allowed experimentation on the new ideas, as indeed had occurred when he suggested the ideas, new at the time, that other members felt had now outlived their usefulness. In this instance, after he had cooled down and reconsidered the situation, and under pressure from the instigator, he eventually agreed to a trial of a less ambitious plan.

The Chairman can also manipulate the meeting by swiftly winding it up, possibly shuffling his papers ready for departure, thus virtually daring anyone to voice dissent, and by ensuring that the record reflects his preferences. Whereas the minutes should be a true and fair record of what transpired at the meeting, since the Chairman is responsible for approving the framing of the minutes, he may be able to change the emphasis or even the meaning of the record. This kind of subterfuge is not unknown and members of meetings need to check that the minutes do actually record accurately what transpired.

CASE STUDY 6.6   A variety of meanings

The Secretary noted the sense of the meeting as:

'In view of the current cash flow position, X and Y were requested to investigate the debtor position.'

When he came to draft the minute, knowing that the Chairman had later stressed the need for urgent action in this area, he wrote:

'In view of the current cash flow problems, X and Y were instructed to chase all debtors in default of payment terms and to report accordingly.'

The Chairman altered this to read:

'In view of the serious cash shortfall, X and Y were instructed to raise £25,000 within a week of the meeting by ensuring all debtors in default of payment terms cleared their outstanding accounts. X and Y were instructed to report to the Chairman regarding this requirement before the expiry of the time allowed.'

———— KEY TECHNIQUE ————

Unless X and Y took notes of exactly what they were required and agreed to do at the meeting, they may be unable to challenge the record, which commits them to both time and financial targets.

The Secretary

A good secretary, like Victorian children, should perhaps be seen and not heard, but must support the meeting administratively, to enable it to perform to its utmost. The Secretary's responsibilities entail the following:

a) generating an agenda in liaison with the Chairman and convening the meeting in good time

b) ensuring, if a quorum is required to be present before the meeting can commence, that at least members satisfying that requirement are present to avoid wasting the time of others attending

c) taking, reporting and recording any apologies for absence

d) checking that members have all the documents required

e) having available spare documents in case members have mislaid or forgotten them

f) ensuring that the meeting's supports, refreshments, note-taking aids, protection against interruption, and so on, are present

g) ensuring that the meeting adheres to and does not overlook any item on the agenda

h) ensuring that those who speak and vote are entitled to do so

i) ensuring that the meeting's decisions are clear and clearly understood by all present

j) noting the sense of the meeting in the minutes

k) keeping the minutes secure and available to members

l) ensuring that action is effected as required by the meeting and reported on at the appropriate time.

Minutes

One of the most important tasks is that of recording accurately the sense of the meeting.

The harassed secretary

Thus the Vice-Chiefs embark on their weekly gavotte
Benignant, bemedalled – they're bonny I wot
As in dapper array around the table they squat
In close consultation. A colourful shot
With keen cut and thrust (carry one and a dot)
They debate: and in stately and circular trot
Go a-chasing of hares from Lands End to John Grot
While trailing red herrings to keep the scent hot
Till out of the hue and cry thus begot
There dimly emerges what's what and what's not
Then they hand out their briefs to the Secretary wallah
(Protesting this isn't a routine they follow)
And leave him to draft and to draft till he's crazy
Minutes and cables, aides-mémoire and précis
And so while the Great Ones repair to their dinner
The Secretary stays getting thinner and thinner
Racking his brains to record and report
What he thinks they will think that they ought to have thought.

(Author unknown but thought to have emanated from a military source in the nineteenth century, this verse was quoted by Sir Arthur Bryant in *The turn of the tide*.)

Whilst included as lighthearted comment, some references in the poem will strike a responsive chord in the hearts of many secretaries, for example, the meeting 'a-chasing of hares' and 'trailing red herrings' may be apposite. The last line is particularly pointed since the Secretary must try to capture in the minutes the sense of the meeting and, as we have seen in Case Study 6.6, versions and memories of this may vary. Writing effective and accurate minutes is an art which must be practised to be improved. They should contain only a résumé of the decisions taken, not the arguments for and against a decision. This is not an inviolable rule, however, and it is for the meeting itself to decide. Minutes must be a true, fair and accurate record, which is particularly important if the meeting needs to produce a certified copy of a minute to a third party, for example, to evidence authority to sign a contract.

After the minutes have been signed by the Chairman as a true record, preferably at the next following meeting, they exist as a record of what transpired and are available for recourse for guidance, evidence and as a source of precedent. However this overlooks the fact that they can be used and, in such use, can help manipulate the meeting and the members. Generally they should contain sufficient information to enable an objective third party to comprehend the decisions taken simply by reading them. Despite the general rule regarding the need to record decisions only, at times it may be necessary, and even advisable, to include additional commentary.

Minutes as action prompts

To ensure prompt action following the meeting the minutes themselves should be prepared as soon as possible and approved in principle by the Chairman. Whether they are then sent immediately to all members is for the meeting to decide. Certainly, if using the minutes as action prompts, they need to go out very quickly otherwise the whole point of the prompt is lost. If the minutes are to be used as action prompts, on each occasion that a member(s) is (are) asked to perform certain work their initials should be placed against the minute covering the item. The minutes then act as both a personalised record of action required and a prompt to the person(s) appointed to carry out the work. They also act to generate peer pressure since the incorporation of initials is a reminder to other members of who is due to carry out the work. In such circumstances X's excuse that 'he didn't realise at the meeting that he was being asked to do the work' cannot stand, though one might have some sympathy for X and Y following the issue of the minutes of the meeting referred to in Case Study 6.6.

Confidante

The Secretary often becomes the confidante of the Chairman, partly since between them they are ultimately responsible for the success of the meeting. This is logical as the Secretary should be impartial and thus able to discuss ideas and concerns with the Chairman from an objective viewpoint. He can also act as a sounding board for the

Chairman's ideas and tactics for gaining acceptance for a piece of business. From his observation of the meeting, he should gain a valuable insight into the views and attitudes of the members of the meeting. With the benefit of this, hopefully impartial, view, the Chairman's own views may be crystallised, possibly prompting him to negotiate with meeting members in advance of the meeting itself, to form alliances, to ensure that objections are dealt with, or to neutralise any opposition.

Useless Chairman

The onus in most of the matters reviewed in this chapter is very much on the Chairman as the leader and motivator of the meeting. Unfortunately it can happen that an ineffective Chairman is appointed, an occurrence more likely to be prevalent in social rather than business meetings but by no means unknown in the latter. Headed (one can hardly say led as it would be a contradiction in terms) by an ineffective Chairman, meetings usually tend to become ineffective and inefficient.

CASE STUDY 6.7   **Raise your voice – raise your responsibility!**

It was obvious that the Chairman had little experience of well-run meetings let alone chairing one. To his despair, the new member found that there was no agenda – merely a list of topics which was actually put together when the members met – no minutes or record of what had been agreed previously, and no apparent intent to address various requirements with any degree of efficiency. In addition, the members of the meeting, lacking any control or leadership, spent virtually the whole meeting chatting amongst themselves rather than addressing the issues they had gathered to discuss. At his second meeting, the new member made several constructive suggestions for improving the performance generally and at his third, the Chairman did not turn up and the new member was asked to chair the meeting.

Sadly such a situation is not always as easily resolved. Often the meeting needs to soldier on, with the Secretary and members trying to push for greater efficiency and performance against the one person who should be leading them in that endeavour!

CHAPTER SEVEN

Cabals and cannibals

Key learning points

- It is vital to identify any pre-determined outcome and manoeuvre the meeting towards it

- Consider likely opposition and analyse anticipated reactions

- Endeavour to understand the requirements of any opposing members and work to circumvent or overcome these

- Neutralising the opposition may be more effective and easily accomplished than overcoming them

Pre-determining the outcome

Experience indicates that it may be necessary to remind some meeting members of their purpose, even if only to act as a criterion against which to measure progress or lack of progress. However, aims may be couched in quite general terms. For example the aims of a Board of Directors may be such as that set out in Fig. 7.1.

- To act as stewards for the owners' investment and property.
- To maximise return on the investment accepting a [pre-set] degree of risk.
- To comply with all legal requirements.
- To maximise the use of employees, providing training when required by the individual and in accordance with the needs of the business.
- To expand the business [by pre-set criteria].

Figure 7.1   Outline Board aims

Obviously these are long-term aims and assume the existence of the Board, and the organisation, for a number of years, during which the aims themselves may not need to be changed. Despite the existence of these long-term guidelines, short-term problems and opportunities will require the development of separate aims. The essence of meeting work is consensus, that is decisions are usually arrived at in unanimity. Seldom is there a need to vote which, by definition, indicates dissent or disagreement amongst the members. Indeed, if there is constant dissent, then it is unlikely if the committee or meeting can be effective or even survive to achieve its long-term aims. As Abraham Lincoln stated: 'a house divided against itself cannot survive'.

With this background meeting members dedicated to a particular item of business may wish to establish a pre-determined outcome, that is to determine the ultimate decision in advance of the discussion. Obviously a member, or the Chairman, who has worked with the same body for some time, will have a fairly good understanding of the meeting members and how they think and react. Thus, they should be able to assess with a fair degree of accuracy how they will view each item of business. Obviously there can still be surprises, but generally an astute and perceptive member can rely on such instincts, whilst always being prepared for an upset.

CASE STUDY 7.1   **Taken for granted**

In Case Study 2.2, the Chairman was effectively abusing his position in trying to force through a policy. His mistake was to assume that he could carry other members of the Board with him, rather than considering their possible views objectively and then considering if there was any way in which they could be won over to his point of view. In fact his knowledge of the reaction of at least one of his colleagues should have indicated at the outset that he was unlikely to make any progress.

——— KEY TECHNIQUE ———

When trying to force through such an item, canvassing support in advance is essential.

Cabals

One of the most widely known meetings is that of the weekly UK Cabinet. The government actually comprises far more ministers than the twenty or so who form the Cabinet, which is thus an 'inner core', the composition and size of which is designed to try to ensure swift progress. This manner of working started under Charles II who, after the restoration of the monarchy, wished to move away from the previous method of government by an overlarge Privy Council and preferred to use a small body of just five trusted advisers. The initials of the first five advisers were C, A, B, A, L which form the word 'cabal', which in turn has come to mean a secretive part of a larger whole; whilst the word 'cabinet' comes from the French word for a small private room in which, presumably, the six persons of King and 'cabal' could be accommodated easily. The possibility of the existence of a cabal within the larger body of a committee must not be overlooked, or unsuspecting members, not privy to the separate deliberations of the cabal, may find themselves ambushed. Indeed, it is not too long ago that a British Prime Minister found herself ambushed in a similar way.

The Prime Minister in question was Margaret Thatcher who found her support in the Cabinet and party insufficient for her to continue in office. Not that this kind of experience was new to her. As John Campbell records in his book *Edward Heath – A Biography* (Cape 1993), when Margaret Thatcher was a minister in Edward Heath's Cabinet, the animosity between the two led Heath to position her at the far end of the Cabinet table and on the same side as himself. Eye contact was thus impossible and it was said that Heath never asked for her views, except at the end of a discussion when he was shuffling his papers ready to move to the next item on the agenda. To counter this, sometimes Mrs Thatcher would request another member to raise business for her, trying to out-manipulate the manipulator.

Cabals have considerable power, particularly if they include the Chairman. After all if two or three members consistently side or support the Chairman there is in existence a bloc of power which it will take considerable opposition to defeat. Whilst not advocating the creation of a cabal, there is no doubt that at times it can be effective, particularly in working towards a pre-determined outcome.

Cannibals

Inherent in pre-determining an outcome is a requirement to consider the means by which such outcome can be achieved. In trying to move towards this outcome the Chairman, or indeed any other member since all may have pet projects to broach for approval, must consider the realities of the situation. In most committees, business needs the support of a bare majority of the members to gain approval. However, experience indicates that many members tend to forget this basic point or think alternatively that the more forcibly they argue, or the louder they demand, very often the more chance of success. This is a little like one of Aesop's fables in which the sun and the wind vie to make a traveller remove his overcoat. The wind uses all the forceful power at its disposal but the effect is only to make the traveller draw his coat ever closer round his body. The sun simply shines, and the traveller swiftly removes his coat, the moral being that persuasion is better than force. Nowhere is this perhaps more demonstrably the case than in the United Kingdom. There is a facet of the British personality that determines that the more one shouts and raves, or even uses force, the less one is likely to succeed.

CASE STUDY 7.2   **Do it my way – or else …**

The Sales Director had a very aggressive personality which was a constant problem in meetings, although he was very effective at his job. He had a complete belief in his own infallibility and ability to force everyone to agree with him, as had

---

occurred at a number of board meetings. At one meeting, however, he was determined to ensure that a pet project of the Chairman, a new product somewhat disrelated to the core products of the company, was cancelled, and argued very forcibly against its continuation. Unfortunately he allowed his own eloquence, anger and belief in his personal power and infallibility to carry him to the point where he stated that unless it was cancelled he would resign forthwith. To his astonishment the Board proceeded to endorse the project and, simply to maintain face, he was forced to offer his resignation. Even then he believed that his offer would be waived, but to his utter chagrin it was accepted and the Chairman, and rest of the Board, who had grown increasingly tired of his tantrums, forced him to set a date on which such resignation would come into effect.

—————— KEY TECHNIQUE ——————

Never threaten or bluff unless you are prepared to have your bluff called.

Confrontation

It is dangerous to assume that one will always be dealing with reasonable people. If other meeting members are determined to gain information or to move to a particular outcome, they may be prepared to use any tactics that occur in order to achieve their ends.

CASE STUDY 7.3   **No time to eat**

The Director was to some degree flattered to be invited to the company's financial advisers' offices for a lunch but was disconcerted to find on his arrival that rather than a private lunch with the single contact, no less than four partners were present. This put him at a considerable disadvantage, not least because he hardly had time to digest the excellent lunch! The aim of the advisers was to pump him

►

for information about his company and since he was outnumbered, they could consider his answers individually and come back at him in turns. Since the information they sought was confidential, he had to spend considerable time fencing and attempting to outwit their penetrating questions!

Perception

Essentially this comes down to having a good perception or understanding of people – easy to say and sadly not so easy to achieve, still less apply. Yet in attempting to move colleagues or meeting members to a pre-determined outcome or desired result, it is essential that their views and opinions, prejudices and preferences, attitudes and previous reactions are all taken into account to guide one to tactics likely to gain their support. If this approach sounds as though it has political overtones, that is hardly surprising, after all politics has been defined as the art of the possible, and what is being suggested is that those who have determined a particular outcome then need to consider how to move others to their way of thinking.

An old saying runs: 'the reason we have one mouth and two ears is so that we can listen twice as much as we talk'. Sadly, in practice this tends to be the exception, and is aggravated by the passive state of hearing being mistaken for the active state of actually listening to what a person is saying. Indeed, active listening requires us to consider not just what a person says, but also what they do not say, and what can be inferred from body language, attitudes and actions. After all a person is quite capable of a multiple response to a given situation. He may well reply to the same question in totally different terms to his boss, his colleagues, his subordinate and his mates and his wife, whilst all the time keeping his real feelings strictly to himself! Perception requires us to try to understand those real feelings, and ignoring such feelings may ultimately provide us with a problem in achieving a pre-determined outcome.

Conditioning the opposition

If member A is able to perceive the other party's viewpoint, or to visualise events and suggestions through their eyes, this can be a valuable tactic in his in-meeting approach. Recognising what the other party seeks allows him to consider providing it.

CASE STUDY 7.4   **Caveat emptor**

The Director was attempting to sell a small business, demand for which was patchy and, at the time of the negotiations, virtually non-existent. In arranging to meet a potential purchaser, the meeting was deliberately arranged towards the end of the working day, but to give the impression of a bustling business the Director arranged contacts to telephone 'enquiries' through to the business whilst the purchaser was present. In addition, in running though an outline of the business, the Director had a checklist with ticks against each item. As he went through the items with the purchaser, he cross ticked each item, inferring that there was another purchaser who had already been through the checklist. At a subsequent meeting he arranged to be interrupted by the other 'purchaser' to provide a degree of urgency to the negotiations.

———— KEY TECHNIQUE ————

Whilst none of these contrivances were referred to or mentioned to the purchaser, they provided impressions to manipulate his interest.

Neutralising the opposition

This does not imply that those wishing to promote certain items of business should bring in the heavies or recruit James Bond, even though at times one can perhaps be forgiven for the thought crossing the mind! It is merely a recognition that in order to win the 'bare majority' for attainment of the outcome, taking out an adverse vote can be a valuable ploy. In determining the outcome and considering methods of moving to that position, the experienced meeting member must consider the opposition and identify ways of overcoming a combined position as separate entities.

Obviously it is not always the case that all those identified as potentially against the business will have the same attitudes or reactions, or even feel equally strongly about the item. Whilst it may be impossible to shift some members to a position of support, handled correctly or appropriately others may be capable of being moved to a position of neutrality. Neutralising some of the opposition can be as valuable as winning support. After all, if the meeting consists of six members and the subject proposer has assessed that two colleagues will be in favour whereas three will be against, all he has to do is to neutralise one of the opposition and he can carry the day, three votes to two. Rather than wasting time on those unlikely to be moved he should concentrate his efforts on the one he feels he can neutralise.

How this can be effected will depend upon the circumstances, but in a long-running committee there are bound to be occasions when the lines of battle contain different members. D, who finds himself against A and B and is considering neutralising C on this occasion, may find himself with B and C and against A, E and F the next time around. Agreeing to support C on another matter in return for his abstaining on the matter in hand is not only sensible from D's point of view but is part and parcel of meeting tactics.

CASE STUDY 7.5   **Prepare the ground first**

In Case Study 6.5. the instigator of the business almost invariably supported the Chairman on other items. Although the Chairman made the mistake of losing his temper, the instigator and his supporters also made a mistake in springing the item of business on the Chairman.

———— KEY TECHNIQUE ————

Had they briefed him prior to the meeting, they might have been able to gain, if not his support, then at least his agreement to letting a trial go forward. The Chairman would then have been in a win:win position. If it succeeded then, as Chairman, he was ultimately responsible for a correct decision, whilst if it failed, it was the instigator's plan to which he had given only tacit consent.

Avoiding adverse reactions

Case Study 7.5 highlights a situation which will be covered later in more detail – the ambush. This occurs either where an item of business is sprung on a committee, or where an alliance of members with majority voting power unexpectedly raises such an item safe in the knowledge that its success is assured, both from the fact that support has already been canvassed and that opposition will be unprepared and unable to combat it effectively. The ambush is effective where support is assured but less so where the case needs to be argued, particularly if this is necessary to win over support. In these circumstances negotiations, or at least exploration of the case, in advance of the meeting may be advisable. Few people like losing out or ending up on the wrong side, particularly in a public forum, and such public defeat may be avoided by broaching the subject with colleagues in advance, gaining their reactions and either toning down or altering aspects of the suggestion or, if there seems to be little support or total animosity, dropping the idea altogether.

Such a strategy has a number of advantages:

- it grants the member the reputation of being a good team player. Reputation and respect can help win arguments in meetings and dealing with a possibly controversial matter outside the meeting, particularly if it concerns or is raised with the Chairman, may well earn the instigator some prestige for future use, even though the actual subject matter gains no support on the present occasion;

- it avoids embarrassing the person with whom it is raised as it could were it to be raised in open meeting, which may give the instigator a slight edge in other circumstances. The position of that person, particularly if he is the Chairman, is thus protected. He can explain opposition or reaction in private, and possibly even in confidence, to the instigator, without the pressure of the meeting;

- it enables the instigator to gain some measure of the depth of feeling likely to be encountered were the matter to be raised in the meeting. If the reaction is very hostile he can back off immediately, excusing himself with some reference to it being an idle thought or even an idea that someone else had mentioned to him!

- the concept itself is brought into the open. Whilst it may not gain support this time around, repeated references to the idea may ultimately win over those formerly antagonistic to it, particularly if later events are used to illustrate its advisability.

CASE STUDY 7.6 **Chinese water torture**

A new Director wanted to introduce a comprehensive personnel administration system which he had originated and used at his previous company. The reaction when this was mooted at the Board was very adverse. 'Seems like a lot of red tape' was one of the kinder comments passed. Subsequently it was discovered by the auditors that due to the current haphazard system, five employees had been over-paid and it would be difficult to reclaim the overpayments. Outside the meeting, the Director pointed out to the divisional Managing Director that his system required Director authority for all payments and incorporated a complete audit path. Using the criticism from the auditors as added ammunition, he gained the MD's approval to the concept and thus raised it again at a Board meeting where, this time around, it gained acceptance.

———— KEY TECHNIQUE ————

In Chinese water torture, water is dripped steadily and constantly onto the sufferer eventually wearing away their resistance, and often their life. Similarly, initial rebuffs should not necessarily deter a member from trying again when circumstances may be more favourable.

Gaining the sense of the meeting

The personalities of meeting members vary considerably. Some will find it easy to contribute to the discussion, to make their points and to debate the subject matter. Others, no less experienced or talented, find it difficult to perform well in a meeting. Repeated attendance, as well as practice and observance of how other members make their contributions should assist them to marshal their thoughts and evidence and to make their case, nevertheless some members still find it hard going. This is particularly true when there are very strong personalities present, as many will fight shy of an encounter with such powerful opponents. The Chairman has a vital role to play in trying to coach the less extrovert to make a contribution. When stronger players threaten to overwhelm the discussion, the Chairman should wait for a suitable pause and then invite someone to make their point, ensuring as he does so that adequate time is given for the point to be made and that the rest of the meeting listens.

There is an inherent danger in adopting this tactic, that is that the Chairman might catch the 'quiet party' unprepared, which could make the situation worse. However this could be covered by the Chairman letting it be known in advance that he would require to hear the contributions from all members, or even briefing members personally. The Chairman's experience should enable him to appreciate that some members have speaking problems. In the event that the members still find it difficult to express their views, the Chairman may have to try to put their views into words for them.

CASE STUDY 7.7 **That's what I meant**

The Sales Director whose demise was recorded in Case Study 7.2 was a very dominant personality at executive meetings, so much so that very often he tended to stifle other members merely by the force of his personality. The Chairman was concerned to obtain input from members and spent some time at each meeting encouraging other members to comment even where their views were diametrically opposed. He invited comments on the Sales Director's suggestion that the development committee be placed under his own responsibility, and some were made, albeit robustly challenged by the Sales Director himself. There then followed a silence although several members had not commented. The Chairman was particularly concerned not to be seen as the focal point for opposition and to obtain the input from a Non-executive Director who was attending, he invited his comments. 'I am not sure this is the forum for this discussion,' was his only reply. The Chairman pressed him to explain further. 'I will be pleased to do so but I want a few minutes to expound several points'. The Chairman immediately ruled, without referring to the committee, that this was acceptable and invited the Non-executive Director to put his case, which was, first, that such a change should be discussed at the Board not at the executive committee, and, second, that it was important that development received both funds and close attention from the Board and thus should remain where it currently reported, to the Chairman.

--------- KEY TECHNIQUE ---------

In that instance not only did the Chairman deliberately throw the conversational ball to a person that he felt might be an ally but who might be reticent about speaking as he was a guest at the meeting, and indeed had no executive power in the company, but also he avoided the possibility of another head-on confrontation with his Sales Director which had occurred previously.

Temperament

Normally meetings proceed smoothly with efficiency and achievement if there has been adequate preparation and planning. Occasionally, however, business is required to be discussed which raises strong feelings and polarises attitudes. In this situation it is all too easy for tempers to be lost and for what would normally be a rational discussion to degenerate into a heated argument, in which case carefully prepared and cogently argued cases are abandoned and a slanging match may develop. In this kind of situation it is essential for the Chairman to assert control and to call the proceedings to a halt, either temporarily, that is for a recess of say 15 minutes, or more permanently, until a later date. Requiring parties to break off the encounter should give everyone a chance to cool down and for their normal tolerance and good humour to be re-asserted. It may also provide an opportunity for emissaries to visit both camps to test the possibility of some kind of mutually acceptable compromise being developed.

CASE STUDY 7.8   **Better to resign ...**

The company was in serious financial difficulties and some members of the Board believed that, whilst the UK recession had not helped, part of the responsibility was that of the Managing Director in whom various members no longer had any confidence. This had been exacerbated by shareholders offering to put more money into the company on the proviso that the Managing Director was replaced. The Board meeting had become stormy with recriminations and accusations being made.

Eventually, realising that no progress was being made, the Chairman ordered a 10-minute recess during which a Non-executive Director spent considerable time with the Managing Director trying to convince him that he would be better resigning as Managing Director whilst remaining as a Non-executive Director, rather than pushing the Board to the limit of firing him. The point was also made that this would be in the best interests of the company as it would allow new funds to come into the company and the Board to concentrate on trying to retain the company's former profitability. Eventually this was agreed. The same emissary then returned to the other Board members suggesting that if the Managing Director was allowed to remain as a Non-executive Director a resignation could be obtained.

———— KEY TECHNIQUE ————

When tempers are roused polarisation of positions occurs and it can be very difficult to see alternatives, as the participants become conditioned by increasingly irate responses. Calming down and thinking without emotive comments or interruptions can encourage new ideas or compromises.

CHAPTER EIGHT

Tactics and strategies

Key learning points

- The desired result of the meeting must always be kept fully in mind, and every attempt made to move the discussion, argument, meeting, and so on, towards it

- Dealing with temper and inflexibility takes patience, whilst responding in a like manner will be self-defeating

- Non-achievers must be dealt with firmly, guiding them to achieve or else requiring their replacement

- The need to distinguish between aggressive and assertive members, and to protect submissive members, is important

An eye on the target

The essential need for meetings is to ensure that they move towards the accomplishment of their aims. However, the aims of the members may not always be in harmony with the aims of the meeting and the Chairman needs to be aware of the possibility of some members attempting to subvert the meeting's aims. Almost inevitably conflict will then arise, although, as already noted, should the Chairman be aware of the situation in advance he may be able to avoid conflict by means of advance meetings, or even by making member or multi-member deals.

Of course the meeting is more important than each individual meeting member, and should also be bigger than the sum of their experience and talent, inferring that each may need to sublimate his or her own particular views and preferences to the requirements of the meeting. Unfortunately, whilst this is sound in theory, not everyone tends to regard their contribution in the same way, and some will attempt to hijack the meeting to attain their own ends. The exposure and outwitting of the impact of such 'hidden agendas' is essential if the meeting is to continue to move towards its aims.

CASE STUDY 8.1   **Prioritise**

At a time when the company's overwhelming aim was to achieve and even beat the year's budgeted sales, the Sales Director was very keen to develop a new agency agreement with a new direct agent in Canada, which, it was suggested, could become a major export market. The small volume of exports had so far been handled via indirect agents overseas who bought the company's product on their own account before selling it onward. The new relationship would mean a sole and appointed agent ordering the goods, but paying for them only once he had sold the goods on. The Chairman was uneasy about the arrangement and could not avoid a nagging concern that there was something behind the Sales Director's enthusiasm.

A meeting was convened specially to consider the project, but before it dealt with the draft contract, the Chairman requested the latest home market projections with an area-by-area analysis of firm and expected sales for the rest of the year. This showed that home sales were seriously under-performing their budget. Accordingly the Sales Director was instructed to postpone the Canadian deal, which was only budgeted to contribute about 5 per cent of annual turnover, and to concentrate on generating additional sales to cover the shortfall in the home market.

———— KEY TECHNIQUE ————

The key here is the need to prioritise. Failing to address this need is a common failing of meeting members as many find difficulty in identifying which matters should receive priority treatment and which should be relegated. This can lead to the situation where a meeting may, unless controlled and directed, spend half an hour discussing a colour for the refurbished bike shed, whilst the unacceptable level of debtors in default of their payment dates, which threatens the whole existence of the organisation, goes unremarked, or at least undiscussed. The problem is often that, whereas the former requires little examination and comes down to personal preference on which all can express an opinion, the latter requires careful study of a far more difficult topic. Left to a choice between the two, the colour of the bike shed is a far safer bet for discussion!

Addressing the problem

In seeking to concentrate on the priorities, the Chairman needs to develop both short-term tactics needed to ensure a particular item or meeting moves towards their desired results, and strategy, to ensure that the meeting and series of meetings as a whole move towards attaining their aims. Inherent in the need to attain aims is a need for action. Action is required from each meeting member and to this end the Chairman must make each member accountable, not excepting himself when appropriate. However the best use of the Chairman's time is usually ensuring that other people are working towards the pre-determined outcome. This must include non-achievers, who are not merely a negative force in terms of a lack of progress, but who are also a considerable demotivating force on their colleagues. Any excuses put forward may be varied but need challenging and defeating so that they cannot be re-used and either action is stimulated or a further excuse is generated. Obviously, if the latter, this may ultimately lead to the replacing of the offender. To concentrate the mind of all members at each meeting, it is therefore good practice for the first items of the agenda to be:

- to note the long-term aims of the meeting
- to note the immediate aims of the subject matter, and then to ensure all discussion leads to the furtherance of those aims.

This sets criteria to which, in the event of non-achievement or distraction, the Chairman can refer in order to bring the meeting back on course.

CASE STUDY 8.2 **Sorting out the priorities**

The Chairman was under considerable pressure from a number of external sources but had agreed to a meeting to discuss new personnel contracts with the Personnel Director and an external consultant who had drafted the new contracts. As a result of the re-drafting, changes to benefits had been suggested, as well as the introduction of controls, particularly over absenteeism. The Chairman commenced by stating that he understood the contracts were needed to comply with new legislation and wished to concentrate on this. In discussing the proposed wording however, the Personnel Director started to become very involved in the new controls on monitoring absence until the Chairman, who knew it was a pet theory and did not wish to hear the same recital again, interrupted to point out that, as had been stated and agreed, that was not the purpose of the meeting, but a side effect to be discussed in another forum. He accepted it might need Board consideration but at a later date and then only following the production of a post-investigation report.

Dealing with excuses

If dealing with non-achievers, inevitably there will be occasions when work required or requested will not be available. Whilst this is acceptable, if crises or other priorities have intervened, all too often excuse is being sought for inefficiency. The Chairman needs to differentiate between the genuine reason and the fraudulent excuse, ensuring that a new date is set in the former instance, and both a new date and a commitment requirement for the latter.

- **'I didn't know you wanted it now.'** This implies self-criticism, since any responsible member should instinctively know when data is required, or at least have the sense to ask. The argument can be countered by laying down the time limits for every item required to be discussed at the meeting and explaining the implications that flow from the non-appearance of such data, that is the inability to make decisions, delay to projects and disruption to progress, and so on.

- **'It's not our department's responsibility.'** In the case of regularly produced data this can hardly be accepted. If there is genuine misunderstanding regarding the provision of data this must be rectified immediately. Basically, throughout the organisation it needs to be made absolutely clear who is responsible for what and when.

- **'No one authorised me to proceed.'** Again, if true, the authority process needs to be reconsidered, sorted and clarified. This is a far more widely experienced problem than is often realised, with problems of both commission and omission. To ensure that meeting members, and others, know their authority and responsibility, a combination of authority chart, such as that shown (in part) in Fig. 8.1 and detailed departmental and job descriptions should clarify and delineate the situation and avoid this excuse being used in the future.

Authority levels   **Organisation name**

It is essential for the proper control of the money and stock assets of the organisation, that authority is granted at, and only at, the appropriate level in order to incur expenditure or approve the disposal of stocks other than in the normal course of trade.

Contracts

All contracts between the company and third parties, other than those covered by items set out below, must be channelled through the Company Secretary's office, to ensure correct status (i.e. whether it is to be regarded as a Deed or not) and approval. The Company Secretary will arrange the passing of suitable Board resolutions granting approval to specified person(s) to sign on behalf of the company. It should be noted that sufficient time to obtain such a resolution should be allowed.

Cash commitment

Capital projects:

Authority for all projects (note: no low cutoff)	Board
(All items must be supported by a Capital Expenditure (Capex) form)	
Repairs and renewals, purchase of furniture and fittings	
(All items must be supported by a Capex form)	
Up to £1000	Manager – level
Over £1000 and up to £5000	Director
Over £5000	Board
Vehicles	
(Supported by Capex form, for new allocations, or Replacement	
form, (for write-offs and replacements)	Board
All purchases to be in accordance with Policy	

[and so on for every item requiring control]

Issued by Finance Director on [date]. To be updated six monthly.

Figure 8.1   Organisation authority chart (extract only)

Whilst the extract shown in Fig. 8.1 is financially orientated, there is no reason why it could not be extended so that it covers general duties and responsibilities similar to an organisation chart, bearing a complete run down of responsibilities.

- **'I'm so busy I just can't get round to it.'** There is an old saying that if you want something done you should ask a busy person to do it. If this is so, then this type of excuse tends to be used by people who are unable to organise themselves, irrespective of the amount of time at their disposal. Whilst some patience may be necessary, if repeated, the bluff needs to be called by a suggestion that, in that case, there will need to be a reallocation of duties, or ultimately that it may be necessary to change the job occupant, any suggestion of which may help concentrate the mind wonderfully. The P45 can be a very good motivator.

- **'We've always done it that way.'** If this is used to explain why data has not been submitted in the way required by the meeting, it may be a genuine response but infers either a lack of attention to, or a lack of clarity in, the original request. In this instance, the need is to ensure that the requirements of the meeting are set out with utmost clarity. Lack of comprehension of what was required cannot then be used as an excuse.

- **'I forgot.'** Hopefully this kind of excuse will be experienced rarely. The immediate counter is to ensure that the minutes are clear, incapable of misinterpretation and issued promptly. They must also specify a time to ensure accountability and be distributed with a covering note stressing the need to comply with items requested. The long-term counter to this excuse may again need to be the replacement of the member.

Temper

The subject here is the loss of temper by the meeting member, not the Chairman, although faced with some of the excuses set out above, the Chairman could perhaps be excused for losing his own temper! However, as the leader of the meeting aiming to achieve its ends, temper or annoyance, other than when 'lost' for deliberate effect, is to be avoided.

CASE STUDY 8.3   **Temper wins the day**

The meeting had been called to discuss the implementation of a promised resignation by a Director once certain events had been put in place. The Director attempted to prevaricate by indicating that his resignation would now take effect only after the calling of a shareholders' meeting. At this the acting Chairman exploded in part real and part sham temper, pointing out in no uncertain terms that this was a real-life situation, that the company was in serious danger of failing and that no one wishing to save it had time to split hairs concerning the manner of a resignation essential to clear the way for a capital restructuring. Such was the vehemence of the reaction from a normally quietly spoken and reserved man, who was also an old friend of the object of his ire, that it was generally agreed to have played a major part in achieving the Director's resignation without further ado.

———— KEY TECHNIQUE ————

Such deliberate loss of temper can be an effective ploy although its repeated use will destroy its effectiveness.

Of greater concern to the Chairman may be the correct reaction when faced with temper or heated arguments between meeting members. The problem is that as the tempers become more and more heated there is usually far less chance of a decision. Reaching a decision is unlikely as compromise is required, and compromise is unlikely given that temper tends to lead, as already noted, to a polarisation of views. Progress is very unlikely to be made when rational thought is impossible. It may be preferable for the Chairman to postpone discussion for, say, an hour, to allow temper to subside, and the parties to discuss the subject matter without emotions inflamed by temper. However, this may be impossible and he may either need to make a ruling or to suspend discussion on the topic.

People react differently when they are seized by temper. Increasing blood pressure can blind some people to rational explanation or logic and often defies attempts at control by a third party. Despite being impartial, intervention by a third party may, in trying to defuse the situation, actually make it worse. The only person capable of re-instating a degree of control is the subject who may be the person least able to do so.

Bearing in mind that any suggestion of deferring consideration until a later time may worsen the situation, calm requests for order from the Chairman, matched by patience and perseverance may begin to calm the situation. Some of the actions in the checklist Fig. 8.2 may also help.

---

1 Remain calm at all times. Once two tempers clash then it is unlikely that any consensus will emerge, and the situation will almost certainly degenerate.

2 Note facts or opposing views without immediately commenting on them. Hasty comments may merely inflame the situation, whilst the longer the member, or more than one member, can talk without being challenged, the more they may be able to reduce the pressure they feel. It is essential to try to ensure that members speak separately and wait, without interrupting, until the other has finished.

3 Keep the member(s) talking and explain the cause of the loss of temper, whilst asking neutral questions to try to uncover as much of the case, or cause of concern, as possible. This may help, simply from the genuine interest being evinced.

4 Attempt to further relax the members by means of refreshment, allowing smoking, or even declaring a recess or adjournment. Care should be taken not to denigrate the concern or infer that the dispute is not serious. The purpose of adjournment is to allow time for reconsideration, or thinking time, and not to stifle the matter.

5 Provide refreshments, thereby diverting attention to a neutral act, as this may provide valuable calming time.

6 On resumption or after the initial flow has ceased, if no adjournment has proved possible, re-check and correct the facts as already discovered and noted. This should enable a more accurate résumé of the dispute to be prepared. Further, since time will have passed since the original outburst, a more objective view may be obtained. This process can be built upon by the Chairman questioning suspect facts or opinions, and challenging suppositions and claims where these appear to be unsubstantiated.

7 Leave as much time as possible for the calming process. Points 1 to 5 may require as much as 30–40 minutes. Indeed, the longer the time taken the better, as the more likely it is that tempers may subside.

8 If an adjournment is possible, this should give the Chairman time to investigate the case.

9 In making a decision under pressure, care should be taken to avoid making precedents and thus decisions should be of an interim nature pending final clarification and/or approval.

10 If an interim decision is implemented, a date and time should be set for review of the matter and implementation of a final decision.

Figure 8.2 Handling temper checklist

Laying down the law

Of course, should temper be a repeated occurrence, then the Chairman may need to stipulate that such reactions are not to be countenanced in meetings, and should this happen the meeting will automatically be suspended. This unfortunately will not deter some members from trying to exploit a situation, particularly if there are other members who have difficulties in expressing themselves clearly regardless of the state of their temper.

CASE STUDY 8.4 **People in glass houses ...**

The Export Manager was furious and at a divisional Board meeting made a vehement attack on the Personnel Manager for apparently disclosing confidential information about him outside the company. Such was his anger, his stream of emotive language and the apparent strength of his case, that the Chairman and other members became committed to the correctness of it. The new Personnel Manager was somewhat taken aback at the combined attack and allowed the complaint to pass virtually unchallenged. However, after the meeting, he sought a meeting with the Chairman, pointed out that the company was legally obliged to provide the information, which concerned the number of days spent outside the United Kingdom by the Export Manager himself. This data had been disclosed to the Inland Revenue and he could not be party to any cover up of such information. The Chairman agreed and added a rider to the minutes of the meeting setting the record straight. Needless to say the episode hardly endeared the Export Manager to the Personnel Manager.

———— KEY TECHNIQUE ————

Of course the Export Manager raising the point should have declared the fact that he personally was interested in the item. Declaring an interest may be required in some meetings where it may have the effect that the person may then not be allowed to speak or vote on the subject. Even if not, it alerts other members to the awareness that views expressed may not be entirely objective.

Encouraging contributions

In this example the aggressor was, at least initially, able to grab the initiative and obtain a decision. At fault was the Chairman for failing to remember that as well as attempting to attain the aims of the meeting and the subject, he was also required to act as referee and ensure that both sides of an argument were heard *before* any decision was made. Another function of the Chairman is to act as leader, in which role he must not stand back at a time of such conflict, but make his presence felt so that all members of the team know that they are being supported. This did not happen here. As the newly appointed Personnel Manager was left floundering under a totally unexpected and heated personal attack made in public, he was entitled to have expected the Chairman to have remained neutral, at least until the facts were known, rather than allowing the meeting to be manipulated. Conversely, the Chairman should have pressed the Personnel Manager for his 'side' of the story either in the meeting or during a short recess, which might have allowed at least one temper to subside. Further, knowing the character of the Export Manager, the Chairman should have requested that he be shown the facts outside the meeting before any decision was made.

Assertiveness versus aggression

The attack outlined in Case Study 8.4 was effective and based on aggression. As such it should have been curbed by the Chairman on that basis alone. What was needed and what would have been perfectly acceptable was an assertive argument or presentation. Unfortunately the two are often confused. The effective Chairman or meeting member needs to be able to both differentiate and ensure that it is assertiveness that is accepted and aggression that is ruled out of order.

The aggressive person makes points and arguments very forcibly, which may be acceptable, but in a way that challenges or destroys the rights of the target to respond, which is not. This attitude employs the 'pre-emptive strike' philosophy, assumes that no other views are feasible and, consequently, that other views should be dismissed out of hand. Conversely, if similar tactics are used on the perpetrators, they tend to try to evade responsibility by blaming others.

On the other hand, the assertive person may make the same points and arguments in an objective way without challenging or destroying the target person's right to respond, or to hold a different opinion. Assertive people are prepared to listen to the views of others and to respect their right to hold different views, even though they maintain their own view. If in the receiving position they tend to accept responsibility, even though they may offer what they may feel to be acceptable reasons.

There is a further category of attitude which needs to be guarded in meetings. This is the submissive persona. This character accepts everything in a meeting, and outside it. They are unable to make their own points and tend to accept all arguments. They also accept everything that is put on them, even though their workload may increase to unacceptable levels. They simply find it impossible, despite inner qualms, to say 'no'. Chairmen need to watch what commitments such members accept, as ultimately, through sheer weight of work they may lose effectiveness and may even explode if the weight becomes too great.

Chairman: We need a report on this matter prepared within the next 48 hours, can you do it?

Submissive: I suppose so, I was going to have tomorrow off but I'll come in and do it then.

Aggressive: Not on your life, I'm already snowed under, find someone else.

Assertive: With what I already have to do I can't see how I can possibly fit it in unless I defer something else.

Figure 8.3   Aggression versus assertiveness – types of response

CHAPTER NINE

Manipulation – spiking the opposition's guns

Key learning points

■ Any member can manipulate a meeting – so be prepared

■ Prepare suitable reactions for members attempting manipulation

■ Dissent is not always detrimental but should be carefully assessed

■ The actual positioning of meeting members may assist obtaining desired result.

Manipulation – a two-way problem

As leader of the meeting the Chairman has more power and opportunity to manipulate the meeting and its members. However manipulation, for both positive and negative reasons, can be undertaken by any of the meeting members, and recognition of the disparate needs and preferences of meeting members, as well as trying to discern their possible motivation for using such devices, is vital, to counter, deflect or overcome such tactics.

Hidden agenda

The principle of the hidden agenda is that whilst everyone else believes that they are discussing a subject in order to agree a course of action, at least one member involved in the discussion actually has another purpose in mind which the acceptance of the recommendation, or sometimes even its defeat, will serve. The purpose of the hidden agenda may be connected with the subject matter but may also be entirely incidental to it. Thus in Case Study 8.3, the apparent and public aim was the consideration of the Canadian agency agreement, whereas the Sales Director actually had two hidden agendas. First, he wished to detract attention from the current poor performance of home sales, and second, he liked the concept of providing an attractive location for an occasional, expenses paid 'jolly'!

It may be possible to expose a hidden agenda by pressing the member to say more concerning the case. For example, the Chairman saying, 'Bill, is there anything you would like to add to what we have already heard?', puts pressure on Bill to expose more of his case, and the more a person talks the more likely they are to do so. This process can, of course, be made far more pointed. For example, in the Canadian agency discussion, the Chairman could have asked the Sales Director what would be his attitude to his needing to travel to Canada regularly. More deviously, he could have seemingly agreed to the concept, but then stated that as this was so important an innovation he would monitor the agent's progress in Canada by travelling there himself regularly, thus removing one of the Sales Director's hidden agendas.

CASE STUDY 9.1 **Whose hidden agenda?**

The Board had a problem in that the divisional Chief Executive plainly was not coping with the job. The Chairman knew that some action needed to be taken although he preferred it to look as though it emanated from the Director rather than from the company. He asked the Company Secretary to try to test out the Director's reaction to the possibility of early retirement on grounds of ill health. The Secretary contrived for it to be necessary for him to make a tour of the division's operations with the Director and during their day out steered the conversation to dwell on the advantages of getting out of the 'rat race' of commuting, meetings, reports and so on. When relaxing, during a meal at the end of a long and tiring day, and after some prompting and leading of the discussion by the Secretary, the Director confided that he was unhappy about the present situation and would be only too pleased to go early. The Secretary, satisfied that he had been able to achieve his hidden agenda, informed the Chairman and the deal was done. He subsequently discovered,

> somewhat to his chagrin, that the Director also had a hidden agenda and had wanted to get the idea of his going early to the Chairman and had used the Secretary to put, as he believed, *his* original idea into the Chairman's head!

Even external meetings sometimes can be abused by those with a hidden agenda, to the extent that the attainment of the apparent purpose is completely impossible.

CASE STUDY 9.2   **It's your order I want, not your job!**

The Director had been approached by a headhunting company to see if he would be interested in joining one of their clients. The Director's Board had been considering for some time whether it would be possible for them to diversify into the business in which the headhunter's client was involved. Accordingly, with the knowledge of his own Board, the Director attended discussions to a fairly final stage, 'testing the water' without letting on the purpose regarding the possibility of a link up, whilst pretending that he was interested in the vacant position.

Testing performance

In all meetings, the Chairman tends to have a hidden agenda, that of checking the effectiveness and performance of the various members. Whereas response can be conditioned by the situation, and a glittering performance can be contributed in a one-off meeting, in a series of meetings consistency of performance is under test. Such analysis of members' performance is constant but needs to be objective, since it is possible for a member to perform well solely because he is never tested to the same degree as others.

Devil's advocate

To rectify this, it may be necessary to employ the device known as 'playing the devil's advocate'. In ecclesiastical circles, the status of 'saint' is granted by the process of canonisation, which is begun by means of a very rigorous quasi-legal examination of the proposal. To ensure that this process is carried out with objectivity, one person, known as a devil's advocate, is required to present a comprehensive case against the proposal, putting forward every argument and fact to try to destroy the recommendation, irrespective of their own personal thoughts on the matter. From this original usage the term has come to be used for the process whereby a supporter's belief, resolve, evidence and recommendations are severely tested by someone, who may in fact support the contention, but acts as a dedicated opponent. Not only should such an action lay bare all facets of the case, but also it tests the strength of enthusiasm of the proposer to the subject matter. After all, if the proposer is lukewarm on the idea then it is unlikely, should it encounter problems, that there will be sufficient commitment to overcome such problems. Conversely, if the proposer is seen to be totally committed to the proposal, then the person playing 'devil's advocate' should be encouraged and reassured. If enthusiasm is present then it is likely that obstacles will be tackled very positively, whilst the commitment of the meeting will act as an incentive to most people to work hard for success to enhance their reputation. This twin commitment may provide sufficient support to overcome most obstacles.

CASE STUDY 9.3   **'It will succeed'**

The Director wanted to open a type of franchise. Under such an arrangement the company would take, under an agreement, space within a larger retail unit. His colleague went through the agreement and, with the Chairman, pointed out all the snags, both legal and operational. Having had their objections rejected by the other side, it was felt that the agreement was potentially dangerous. However the Director was adamant that he wished to proceed, and apart from stipulating a more advantageous termination clause, the meeting decided to accept the agreement, 'warts and all'. Since his commitment was so total and he was the one who had to make it work, it was felt that this would overcome operational difficulties.

———— KEY TECHNIQUE ————

The Director put himself under additional pressure by fighting for his preferences with the Board. Failure would mean not just the abandonment of the concept, but would also damage his judgement and reputation.

CASE STUDY 9.4   **'That's what I said – that's the way it will be'**

The Manager had picked up responsibility very late for a building project which had not been controlled well in its early days and was running late. At a meeting, she stated that part of the operation was expected to move on a set date. The Chairman, playing devil's advocate, outlined all the snags that he could see which would militate against this date being achieved, but the Manager remained adamant that as she had stated a date, that would be adhered to. Eventually this was accepted even though the Chairman laid a bet that she would not do it!

Despite a number of problems, the date was achieved, and the bet won, even though the Manager had to enlist the help of her family at the final stage to assist the carpet layers and so on, and to physically move some items, as the deadline neared.

———— KEY TECHNIQUE ————

Having laid her reputation on the line, the Manager's commitment to meeting the deadline was absolute.

Wet blankets

The Managers referred to in Case Studies 9.3 and 9.4 are perhaps the best types of meeting members to have. Their commitment and enthusiasm for a project is total, and their drive engenders success where others would probably fail, or at least not succeed within the timescale allowed. Most people can get it right second or third time, or after repeated delays and deferments, but only a few seem able to get everything together to make it first time. At the other end of what we could call an 'attainment scale' to such achievers, are wet blankets, those who actually contribute very little but simply highlight all the problems, real and imagined, and apparently rejoice in failure. Their stock phrase tends to be, 'I told you that would happen', and because of their essentially negative attitude they may be of little practical help to most meetings. If it is suspected that they are having a demotivating effect on other members and holding back the successful attainment of the aims of the meeting, it may be necessary to replace them. However, dispensing with someone like this should not be automatic, since on occasion their presence may help. For example, should the meeting consist of a number of other very positive and assertive members whose incautious enthusiasm might lead them into areas from which others might hold back, a 'wet blanket' approach might be a useful dampener.

CASE STUDY 9.5   **Doing one's own thing**

The company operated retail units supported by localised warehouses. A new and very enthusiastic Managing Director was appointed and prepared a report calling for a massive expansion of the number of units supported by one central and large warehouse. Projections of capital, personnel required and timings were prepared and the Board generally became very enthusiastic. One member, however, commented that he had always found it very odd that the company was the only one which operated in this way since all its competitors operated on a direct delivery basis. As the same competitors seemed to make better profits, he wondered if it were really correct that the company had it right and everyone else had it wrong. Enthusiasm dampened, the whole strategy was re-examined and instead of the considerable capital commitment in a central warehouse, which was purely a cost centre, the company invested in the acquisition of larger shops capable of taking direct delivery.

———— KEY TECHNIQUE ————

Enthusiasm is invaluable but should not be allowed to overwhelm the need for objective consideration of the basics.

Procrastinators

Whilst the application of the occasional wet blanket may be beneficial, particularly where it causes over-enthusiastic members to stop and think again, procrastinators have few redeeming features. Their stock in trade is to demand that a decision be deferred for what to everyone else may seem to be no good reason, or their performance is such that every time achievement is required they seem to have reasons for its non-attainment. To ensure that their performance, or lack of it, does not detract from the meeting's performance, the Chairman may need to take a close interest in them. This could include:

■ setting accountable targets to try to generate action

■ supporting and guiding them to accomplish what is required of them and

■ constantly progressing chasing until action becomes instinctive and their procrastination a thing of the past.

If their performance does not improve, even with the Chairman, 'riding herd on them', replacement may be necessary. Indeed, the threat of this may actually be used as an additional goad.

Ditherers

Meetings exist to make decisions and meeting members, whilst a balance is necessary, predominantly need to be people who are capable of making up their minds, taking decisions and effecting implementation. Those who find it difficult to perform in this way, and, sad to say, there are people who can neither prioritise nor take decisions, are unlikely to be able to survive the meeting situation. In fairness to them, as much as to their colleagues, they should be substituted as soon as the problem, despite remedial action, seems to be incapable of resolution.

Bullies

The principle of aggression, the tactic implicit in the actions of the bully, was explored in Chapter 8. Whilst endeavouring to change the bully from the aggressive to the assertive mode, if he or she is otherwise an achiever, most meetings may be loath to dispense with their contribution. The approach to the bully could be to:

■ let them explode or pressurise

■ summarise their points, ignoring all emotive aspects, and concentrate on the valid facts

- confront them with alternative facts and contentions without responding to the temper or pressure or

- present the alternative in a way that enables them to save face.

If able to use a face-saving device, an informal word of advice about converting aggression into assertiveness may also help avoid a repetition, particularly if the point is made that next time a face-saver may not be available.

CASE STUDY 9.6   **Pointless aggression**

The discussion between management and trade union had reached a delicate stage. A meeting was convened and a few minutes before the set time, the union representatives arrived at the office and without stopping at reception walked straight to the Boardroom and occupied seats including that normally used by the Managing Director. When the MD arrived to commence the meeting he was infuriated by this total lack of manners and consequently refused all concessions then requested by the union.

_____ KEY TECHNIQUES _____

Whilst a demonstration of strength may assist, unnecessarily 'needling' an opponent achieves nothing and merely creates a backlash.

It should not be overlooked that merely taking a certain seat at a table can make a statement. If, on being shown into a room, a visitor takes a seat at the head of a table, it may indicate that they intend to try to dominate the discussion and are probably more ego-centred than team-centred. Taking a seat along the length of the table can indicate the opposite.

Blamers and moaners

These essentially negative players usually seek to protect their position by sliding away from any accountability and trying to blame others for their own shortcomings in the process. Whilst some opponents seem oblivious or unconcerned at this unsocial behaviour, others can become extremely annoyed. The effect, irrespective of attitude, is that the effectiveness of the meeting is impaired and thus action needs to be taken as follows:

- confront the offenders with any complaints regarding their attitude lodged by their colleagues;
- ensure that the facts of the matter are clearly put forward and that only facts are collected in return (that is, do not allow further blame and moans to be made unchallenged);
- avoid sympathy and force objective consideration;
- turn the argument on to them by requesting from them, their suggestions for the way forward.

Unless positive reaction can be forced from them, it may be necessary to replace them as members.

CASE STUDY 9.7   **Shifting the blame**

The Director, in attempting to help the divisional Chief Executive improve productivity in the continuous shift working factory, had developed the habit of daily 'walking the job', trying to uncover problems and to ensure that they were resolved. After a few weeks he became aware that there were a certain number of problems which seemed to re-occur continually and yet always seemed to be the responsibility of 'the other shift' – each shift manager in turn passing responsibility for problems to the previous shift.

──────── KEY TECHNIQUES ────────

He introduced a shift record in which each Shift Manager was required to enter salient details of output achieved together with a note of problems encountered and steps taken to resolve them. The managers of both adjoining shifts were required to sign the record at each shift. Virtually immediately the animosity died out and understanding and teamwork improved.

Shafters

This description is applied to those who, forsaking any custom and practice, force through a particular piece of business ignoring any effects that it might have on other meeting members. The principle of dealing with the shafter depends on how the original anti-social behaviour was conducted. If there was an ambush or piece of sharp practice then the manner of dealing with it is constantly to refer to it in whatever context seems appropriate, plus perhaps a few that do not. The other meeting members will thus not be able to forget the incident and constant repetition can indicate the strength of feeling about the 'anti-social' behaviour. Sometimes this constant reference has the effect of pressurising the originator of the shaft to apologise for the original action. The last way to react to a shafter should be to 'turn the other cheek' and ignore the action.

Dissent

Most of the types highlighted in this chapter are dissenters in the widest sense of the word. Because they have, in the main, been displayed in negative terms, this does not mean that all dissent must be bad. Some dissent, for example that thrown up by the devil's advocate, can be effective, whilst some is an essential part of achieving a balance of views, and, indeed, a balanced approach to the projects and business. Nevertheless, it is essential that dissent is anticipated, planned for and brought out into the open. If antipathy can be addressed outside and in advance of the meeting, this will not only save the meeting's time, but also enable it to gain from its apparent unanimity and cohesion. It will also gain since the member's public loss of face will be avoided. Many meeting members react with stubbornness if pressure is brought to bear on them in open meeting, particularly if no face-saver is available, although they may be prepared to sublimate their views if tackled in private and in advance. If antipathy cannot be negated in this way, then it must be exposed and addressed within the meeting so that it can be overcome, rationalised or simply outvoted.

Combat

In order to combat potential dissent, the Chairman, or the project proposers, or some-times both, may need to enlist support. This may be either active support from those prepared ultimately to vote with them, or at least tacit support from those not prepared to vote against. In the situation where the meeting is likely to be divided it is essential that such support is not taken for granted, or left to the time of the meeting to determine. Advance canvassing may be essential. After all, the unforeseen can always occur; for example, a member whose support was expected is absent or, worse, totally against the concept.

Applying the random distribution theory, in any selection of 8 or 10 meeting members, 3 or 4 are likely to be in favour of an item of business, 2 or 3 are likely to lack interest one way or another, leaving perhaps 2 or 3 who might oppose the matter. This may actually be too gloomy if one accepts the American research that only six per cent of people refuse to 'get along' in most situations. Although the source of this research is impeccable, the experienced meeting member might wish to question why it is that representatives of that six per cent always seem to congregate in his meetings, since at times dissenters seem far more numerous than this tiny minority would seem to infer!

However, assuming that there may be at least one and more realistically two or three opposers to an item of business, the Chairman should ensure that their strength is dissipated. Obviously seeking them out in advance and endeavouring to neutralise one or more, or to do a deal to gain tacit support may well be possible. But if this is not possible and the level of opposition remains, other steps can be taken. For example, the worst mistake would be to let them sit together at the meeting. If two or three members who oppose the business are seated next to one another, the effect on other members is that the whole seems greater than the sum of the parts. They will appear as a sizable bloc and an effective block on business.

Splitting the bloc

If determined opposition is expected then the meeting should be seated. Aggravation tends to be inflamed if people are standing, and reduced if they sit. This is the principle behind the move to make football stadia all-seaters, as violence is reduced if spectators are seated. Further, seating everyone in very comfortable chairs may also reduce the capacity for opposition. Finally, those who are likely to oppose need to be dispersed, and not to the far corners of the discussion table either as this may enable them to regroup and even solicit support from uncommitted members. If there are three, then at least one, preferably the leader, should be seated very near the Chairman, which may enable the latter to control or even silence his opposition. If the meeting uses the principle of the House of Commons, where before speaking a member has to catch the Speaker's eye, so that to speak the Chairman has to grant permission, even if only by the briefest of nods, then the person located nearest the Chairman will then have the greatest difficulty, by sheer juxtaposition, in catching his close neighbour's eye!

Other opposition members need to be spread amongst supporters of the business (*see* Fig. 9.1). In this way, their apparent strength or weight will be marginalised and they will find it difficult to communicate between themselves, which may be necessary in order to re-group or seek an alternative tactic. In addition, if each is seated next to a strong supporter of the business, the opposition may feel inhibited about making their protest at all, or continuing it in the face of experienced or heavy opposition. This echoes the principle of the appointment of Non-executive Directors to the Board of Directors of public companies. Since one such objective Director, asking questions that executive members least want asked, may feel inhibited about making his presence felt, the recommendation is that at least two should be appointed. In this way they can provide moral and vocal support to each other and become a force with which to be reckoned.

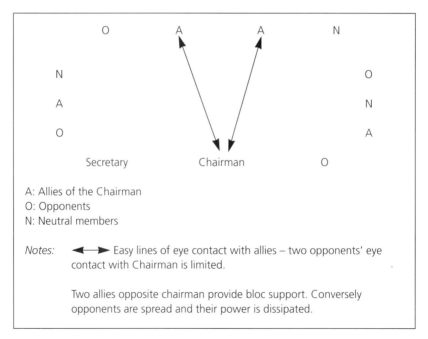

A: Allies of the Chairman
O: Opponents
N: Neutral members

Notes: ◄──► Easy lines of eye contact with allies – two opponents' eye contact with Chairman is limited.

Two allies opposite chairman provide bloc support. Conversely opponents are spread and their power is dissipated.

Figure 9.1   Divide the opposition – and rule

Silencing the opposition

As well as physically splitting the opposition, the Chairman has power to downgrade their contribution by:

- 'not seeing' that they wish to make a contribution and thus not inviting their input
- 'cutting across' their contribution should they stray for one moment from the core of the subject and
- applying 'kangaroo' or 'cloture' motions, restricting comments to a short period.

In addition, the Chairman can allow dissenters too much time so that they start repeating themselves. Allowing too much time can imply that what has been said has not been very telling and it is assumed that they have further points to make. If none can be made the inference is then of an unfinished and possibly insufficiently supported case. Conversely, in allowing a right of reply, the Chairman may allow a supporter more time 'by mistake' to try to counter the case, although advance briefing of this possibility may be necessary.

Should the situation develop where a project thought to be essential for the business is likely to fail due to the activities of the opposition, despite all the steps taken to negate their impact, the Chairman may need to act swiftly to ensure its survival, if not at the current meeting, then at an adjournment or subsequent meeting. In such a situation, the Chairman, anticipating the out-voting and defeat, may need either to withdraw the item, to propose that it 'be left on the table' (that is, held over until the following meeting) or to adjourn the meeting itself. His powers to perform any or all of these acts will depend on the terms of reference of the meeting and it is essential that he is aware of the terms of reference and delineation of such powers.

CHAPTER TEN

Filibusters and tangenteers

Key learning points

- Be prepared for the possibility of the meeting being hijacked by filibusters or tangenteers

- Preparation of a speaker's guide can help focus members' attention and control the length and content of speeches

- Members should avoid laying themselves open to pressure

Dealing with the opposition

Meeting time is precious and even if the acid test referred to in Chapter 1 is not applied, every meeting has costs. Indeed, that test dealt only with time costs whereas there will be others, such as travel, accommodation and so on. Meetings should therefore be advertised as having a pre-set duration. Whilst this helps focus preparation for business and controls the overall meeting length it gives a weapon to one person in particular – the filibuster.

The filibuster

Filibustering entails the use of speech itself as a means of delaying action. It originated as parliamentary tactics in the United States' senate which, unlike the House of Representatives, has no rules over speaking time used. By means of this device, a group of senators, sometimes a sole senator as occurred in 1957 when Senator Thurmond of South Carolina talked for 24 hours, use grossly extended speeches to delay or prevent parliamentary action. They talk for so long that the majority either grants concessions or withdraws or amends the subject matter. Whilst this concept is predominantly used in the context of state legislative bodies, the filibuster can be used anywhere if time is of the essence. The onus in this situation is on the Chairman to try to ensure that the meeting is moved on to discuss the business required. Faced with a filibuster, it may be difficult the first time round to do other than accept the inevitable, but where a filibuster is anticipated, the reactions set out in Fig. 10.1 may be of assistance.

---

1   Implementation of a speakers' guide stating that, for example, only five minutes per speaker will be allowed on each topic, on pain of suspension from the meeting for exceeding the time limit. This could be backed up by a triple colour light indicator. Whilst the green light shows, the person can speak; when the orange light is lit, this indicates that only two minutes' speaking time is left; when the red light begins to flash only 45 seconds is left. When the red light ceases flashing and remains constant the speaker must stop. Power for any microphone used can be linked so that the microphone goes dead as soon as the red light remains constant.

2   An announcement that should the meeting not consider all aspects of the subject matter, it will be adjourned until a set time and date. This can negate the actions of a filibuster, although if a decision is needed urgently, it may be difficult to achieve.

3   An announcement that, whether everyone has spoken or not, a decision vote will be taken at a pre-set time. Whilst ensuring that progress is made, the filibuster can still be effective, as it can deny the supporters of the motion the right or opportunity to make their points.

4   An announcement that only two speeches of (say) ten minutes' duration or less will be allowed from each of the proposing and opposing sides. This rule could also be made subject to the restrictions set out in point 1 above.

Figure 10.1   Tactics for dealing with filibustering

Tangenteers

Implicit in filibustering may be a need to incorporate other subjects into the address as it will be difficult to speak for long enough on one subject to create an effective filibustering speech. Almost inevitably the filibuster will need to deviate from the main subject. This type of approach can also be used by some meeting members either to waste time, or to try to divert the attention of the meeting to a hidden agenda or pet project, or to detract attention from an item on the agenda which the member would prefer not to be discussed or to restrict discussion on such an item.

CASE STUDY 10.1 **Off at a tangent**

The Director had been experiencing great difficulty formalising a number of minor contracts and felt he had gone as far as it was possible to go with many of the opposing negotiators. He knew, however, that this fact would not be given credence with some of the Board who, regardless of the realities of the situation, wanted all of them finalised without further delay and in their favour.

He also knew that the Chairman was in a hurry to end the Board meeting so that he could travel some distance for a business dinner later that evening. He calculated that if he could engineer the meeting so that discussion of the contracts, the last full item on the agenda, was restricted to five or ten minutes before the critical time for the Chairman to leave, he might be able to gain agreement, whereas, if time were left for more detailed discussion, dissent would surface and agreement would be unlikely. Accordingly, when the meeting moved to the penultimate item on the agenda he spent some considerable time watching the clock and the Chairman's growing impatience to get away, expressing his concern at proposals to assign two properties to contacts of the Chairman because of the possible recurring liability to the company under the leasehold property 'privity of contract' rule.

──────── KEY TECHNIQUE ────────

By developing a quite legitimate discussion that, instead of assignment, the company should consider underletting, he managed to occupy all but eight minutes of the meeting's allotted time. He knew he was on to a possible winner when the Chairman started gathering his papers together for the 'off'. True enough, the delay in formalising the various contracts went through virtually 'on the nod' as the available time expired.

Woolly wafflers

The Director in Case Study 10.1 could have been accused of wasting time although the matter that he spent time pursuing at a tangent to the main purpose of the meeting, was nevertheless legitimate and important. This rationale cannot be applied to those who, when requested to report at a meeting, seem totally incapable of marshalling thoughts, facts and recommendations into any kind of order so that a cogent report is prepared. The trouble with such 'woolly wafflers' is that often they have a grasp of the fundamentals of the subject, and indeed may have completed adequate research to enable them to assemble the required data, but they simply cannot 'get it all together', or at least get it together in a way capable of assimilation by anyone other than themselves.

CASE STUDY 10.2 **Good waffling material**

The Training Manager had been delighted when the Board agreed with his proposal to develop a training programme for its staff and spent a considerable time developing the paper work. Before implementation the Personnel Director requested sight of the course notes and was horrified to discover that although aims, practices, checklists and exercises were present, there was no logical progression or order. The lack of a coherent structure would, he felt sure, regardless of the enthusiasm of the presenter, lead to a situation where those on the course could be baffled or confused rather than coached and helped.

A meeting was held with the Training Manager at which he tried to explain the shortcomings without disincentivising the Manager who had obvious enthusiasm for the project. He was unable to make his concerns understood or to engender a more logical approach to the whole course, and so finished up revising the paperwork himself but under the name of the Training Manager.

Leaving the course under the Manager's name and carrying out the work confidentially preserved the Training Manager's commitment. He still regarded the course as 'his' but used the material his boss had developed as a base for his own work. Thus an ideal 'win:win' situation was developed.

Timewasters

Unlike other types so far addressed, timewasters perform their negative act not to divert attention or to ensure that inadequate time is allocated to pre-set business, but simply to please themselves. Such meeting members tend to regard their presence at the meeting as a semi-social diversion, and do not seem to appreciate that the meeting has aims and that results need to be achieved, overriding all social aspects. Accordingly, contributions from these sources tend to be somewhat divorced from reality and usually irrelevant. The Chairman needs to bring such members back to address the business listed and may also need to address the question of whether they should remain members of the meeting at all.

CASE STUDY 10.3   **Timewasting Chairman**

The Chairman of the division was approaching retirement and slowing down. He was a grand old man with a fund of anecdotes and great command of the history of the company, particularly the way it survived the Second World War. Unfortunately, like many of the elderly, his memory for more recent facts and figures was somewhat suspect, and, perhaps because he knew this, he seized upon any reason to launch into a reverie of remembrance of 'how we used to do things' from many years previously as 'guidance' for the present day. Whilst this was entertaining the first few times around, it became increasingly infuriating to the rest of the Board, particularly as the real problems of the division were going undiscussed by the Board whilst it listened to his recollections.

Blackmailers

As meetings comprise a number of members, the opportunities for alliances are virtually unlimited. Where alliances cannot be formed there may be a temptation on the part of one or more members to try to convert the sense of the meeting to support their views by means of blackmail, that is by putting pressure, beyond business requirements, on their colleagues to agree to their pet project.

CASE STUDY 10.4   **Extorting support**

The newly appointed Managing Director was very conscious of his own position and authority and distributed to the rest of the Board his revision of the company profit plan for the remainder of the year. At the meeting held to discuss the plan, which lacked cash flow and pro forma balance sheet projections as well as any rationale for the plan projection, the Managing Director demanded that it be approved by the Board without discussion or amplification of its criteria or basis. The other Directors protested that this was unacceptable as so much was lacking from the plan, but were told that unless the Board accepted the plan as it was, the Managing Director would immediately resign.

——— KEY TECHNIQUE ———

Given that the company was in a serious financial and trading state, the Board had no alternative but to agree to the plan on the basis that it was to be used only as a discussion document with the company's bankers, and the supporting documentation would be prepared forthwith and subjected to proper examination.

CASE STUDY 10.5   **Blackmail for a personal whitewash**

The situation in the company referred to in Case Study 10.4 rapidly grew worse and a shareholders' meeting was convened to discuss the company's apparent insolvency and future, or lack of a future. At that meeting, the same Managing Director tabled a so-called 'plan' for the company's survival which depended upon certain conditions being met. In the introduction to the document, and in his verbal commentary, he stipulated that unless all the conditions it contained were met, he would resign as Managing Director forthwith. Since few, if any, of the conditions were under the control of the Board, the shareholders or the company, it was hardly surprising that some could not be met and thus the Managing Director immediately resigned, using a typed resignation letter he had already prepared. Following his departure from the meeting it was decided that there was no alternative but to request the bank to appoint a receiver. The Non-executive Directors were left to initiate this action, firmly of the opinion that the Managing Director's 'resignation' had been engineered by the deliberate introduction of conditions which were aimed to ensure the creation of an 'impossible' situation for him. The situation, which he had engineered, then 'forced' the implementation of his pre-planned resignation. He gained the advantage that he was no longer in office when the real decision of the meeting, that is the appointment of a receiver, had to be made. Subsequent recriminations could not therefore be aimed at him.

———— KEY TECHNIQUE ————

On some occasions, what is actually blackmail is, in fact, a cunningly disguised means of generating action which will appear to have been initiated by the other party.

Saboteurs

Most members are committed to the interests of the meeting and the attainment of the aims of the meeting, despite at times needing to sublimate their own preferences to the long-term interests of the meeting. At times, however, the depth of feeling on particular issues can be so strong that members would apparently prefer to see the meeting collapse rather than allow it to follow a course of action.

CASE STUDY 10.6   **'I'll bring the whole thing down'**

Following a major Boardroom row, the Chairman and founder of the company had agreed to stand aside and resign. Despite such agreement there was an ongoing argument between him and the rest of the Board to such an extent that he threatened to withdraw his personal guarantees of the company overdraft. The Board pointed out that, were this to take place, and be permitted by the bank, which was unlikely, this would immediately bring about the collapse of the company, the loss of shareholders' and creditors' money as well as the requirement on the Chairman himself to honour such guarantees which his own action would have triggered. Such was his anger, prompted to a large extent by an over-developed ego, that despite the inevitable outcome of this domino effect, he seemed committed to this course of action.

———— KEY TECHNIQUE ————

Usually this kind of attitude will be a bluff and holding firm will call the bluff, which can hardly be repeated.

Political manoeuvrers

This is not meant to refer to meetings held for political purposes but meetings where politicking, that is manoeuvring for personal position or advancement, takes place. Although, refreshingly, it is outlawed (at least in theory) in some organisations, nevertheless it is probably true to state that it is present to some extent in all organisations and can be particularly prevalent in large companies. The Chairmen of meetings where it takes place should make every effort to try to outlaw and out-manoeuvre the manoeuvrers, or the effect will be the dilution of effort devoted to the aims of the organisation in favour of the personal aims of the individuals.

CASE STUDY 10.7 **Position and positioning**

The two divisional Directors were, apparently, good and established friends. To the new divisional Director, however, it was obvious that there was considerable rivalry under the surface of their friendship, as they had both arrived at the presumption that, once the current top management in the group retired, one or other of them should be able to claim the top executive job. He was bemused to be approached first by one, and subsequently by the other to form alliances which would have as aims the damaging of the prospects of the other. This happened both in private in advance of the meetings and on occasion, during the meetings. His reaction to both parties, initially and on all subsequent instances, was that he was not interested in such alliances, and would always speak and vote independently.

———— KEY TECHNIQUES ————

Whilst alliances, and thus reciprocal support, have a superficial attraction, linking one's reputation to another can have serious repercussions.

Further, no matter what the response in this eventuality, the relationship can never be the same again. The person suggesting the alliance has disclosed an attitude to a third party which provides that third party with an advantage. Rejecting the offer, however, may actually damage the position of the third party since thereafter they may be regarded as a threat by virtue of their knowledge of the proposal.

Adverse allies

As noted in Case Study 10.7, liaising with other executives has a potential downside, that is of the ally being disgraced and the taint spreading to those with whom he was associated. Conversely, remaining aloof may preserve an edge of power to the owner of the support sought after. If such support is not guaranteed but merely hinted at, contenders will be left wondering if support from such a quarter might be forthcoming. This could be a considerable help to the non-committed member in trying to manipulate support for his own preferred items of business. This kind of relationship can be termed that of the adverse ally, a person who seems ready to support and yet does not grant full commitment. Taken a step further, such a person may be ready, if not to support the other party at least not to oppose him, or further still to agree on a 'you scratch my back and I'll scratch yours' device. This may entail at least an agreement to lay off the support-seeker's territory in return for the support-seeker laying off one's own area of responsibility.

CASE STUDY 10.8   Mutual lay-off

Having been used to fairly assertive and contentious executive meetings at his previous position, the newly appointed Personnel Director was somewhat bemused to find that the equivalent committee of his new company was a fairly meek and mild concern which rarely seemed to develop any heat or dispute, most reports being taken 'on the nod' or with a minimum of investigation or question, even where a poor performance was obviously evident. As he became more involved and aware of the flow of business he realised that the source of this harmony was the fact that each of his four colleagues headed an operating division and they seemed to have developed, over the years of working together, a tacit agreement that one did not press one's colleagues too hard on their divisions' performances and in return one's colleagues would not press one too hard!

Retaining an open mind

Whilst open dissent must be controlled and channelled, some element of disagreement may be necessary if ideas are to be developed and progress made. If a meeting is becoming cosy and social rather than aloof and examining, or members regard it as an excuse for a social chat rather than an examination of performance and a forum for developing plans and strategy, then the Chairman needs to manipulate the whole endeavour to ensure attention is focused on the essentials needed to be addressed by the meeting. As Shakespeare says in *As You Like It*, 'sweet are the uses of adversity', to which we can reply, 'and beneficial can be its effects in encouraging new ideas, slaughtering sacred cows and challenging established concepts'.

Organisations do not stand still, as they must either progress and expand and live, or stagnate, contract and eventually die. Meetings of the bodies controlling such organisations need to be manipulated if they are not addressing the basic needs of the organisation, in the same way that members need to be manipulated in order to ensure that they do conform to the requirements of the meeting. Thus, ideally all members should come to the meeting with an open mind, although they will almost certainly have preferences. This being the case should not prejudice them from listening to the arguments of others before arriving at a conclusion on the basis of the strength of the arguments put forward.

Obviously this is an ideal and not all meetings, or all members, live up to it, or attain it at all times, as pressures may combine to influence and manipulate the members. Where this is by virtue of the force of his own commitment to the argument this may be acceptable, but where it is due to pressure from an external agency or other member it is certainly not. If the latter is suspected, then investigation should be implemented.

CASE STUDY 10.9 **Underhand pressure**

At the divisional executive meeting the Secretary was somewhat bemused to find the Accountant supporting an argument being made by the Transport Manager for greater flexibility in the disposal of surplus company vehicles. Since the Secretary had doubts over the honesty of the Transport Manager, he was concerned that the Accountant, the person most responsible for ensuring strict compliance with financial procedures and so on, was supporting a relaxation of rules which might prevent the transport function from arranging illicit deals.

After the meeting the Secretary broached the matter with the Chairman of the meeting who had also been concerned but was unwilling to raise it officially. It was decided that the Secretary should do so by means of a friendly discussion, whilst reviewing other matters. The Accountant, in some embarrassment admitted that the Transport Manager, knowing the Accountant's fondness for real ale, had obtained a case of special brew from his previous employers and deposited it in the boot of the Accountant's car the day before the meeting. Whilst no deal had been done and the Transport Manager had not requested support, knowing of this 'gift', the Accountant had found it difficult to do other than support the Transport Manager's suggestion in meeting.

'You do realise that not only have you put yourself in that man's power, Jim, but also it is possible that the beer itself has been removed from his previous employer's premises without their knowledge or agreement, and, if so, you could be held to have received stolen property. Finally, if it turns out that the relaxation of the surplus vehicle disposal system has been used to develop private deals, you could also be held to have been negligent in upholding your responsibility for the application of financial controls.'

The Accountant, who had not realised the full implications of the position, asked for advice.

'Firstly, call the Transport Manager in and say that you want to check the current system. When you come to the suggested relaxation, query it and express concern on the basis that you had not understood the implications, are not happy about it, and need to give it some further thought before agreeing. Then, as the conversation ends, say that when you got home last night you opened your boot and found a case of beer, and ask him if he knows anything of it. If he says it was a gift because he knows you like beer, say that you appreciate the thought but cannot possibly accept the gift and could he remove it immediately.'

_____ KEY TECHNIQUE _____

Effectively the Chairman was able, using a third party, to out-manipulate the manipulative Transport Manager, to remove the threat of pressure from the Accountant and to restore the *status quo* without confrontation or official investigation. This was a serious situation but, even then, some degree of face-saving was felt prudent, particularly as contriving to make the whole thing appear a misunderstanding provided a situation where, hopefully, the Transport Manager's awareness was not alerted to senior management's concerns over his honesty, which were later vindicated.

CHAPTER ELEVEN

Ambushes and assassinations

Key learning points

■ A realisation that not everyone thinks as you do may provide some degree of readiness to deal with ambushes and assassinations

■ Quick and lateral thinking is also needed

■ If a swift defence or response is not possible consider using points of order to gain thinking time

■ The rumour system should only be manipulated with caution

Ambushes

In Case Study 8.4 the attack mounted by the Export Manager was totally unexpected, as the item was not listed for discussion on the agenda. As such, it was an ambush, the target being the Personnel Manager, who was so taken aback that he did not really respond, partly because the consensus of the meeting seemed to be entirely against him, and partly because as a newcomer he was unsure of the company attitude to its compliance with legislation. He felt he could hardly argue the case until he had an opportunity to check the position with the Chairman. Ambushes of this nature can be quite common, particularly should the Chairman be somewhat inexperienced or lack total control which would otherwise outlaw such behaviour. However, the perpetrators of ambushes need to be careful to watch their own flanks as animosity generated by such an attack may well cause a backlash.

CASE STUDY 11.1   **Vengeance**

Despite his vindication in the matter of the Export Manager's UK residence question (Case Study 8.4), the Personnel Manager was, perhaps understandably irritated that rather than come to him for clarification, the Export Manager had broached the subject in open meeting with, it seemed, the direct and sole aim of belittling him in the eyes of the Board. As a result of the incident, he concluded that the Export Manager was not someone who should be trusted, or whose motives could be accepted at face value. Accordingly he tended to give him something of a wide berth and to treat him with caution.

A year later he was astounded to find that against all the company rules the Export Manager had drawn fairly large advances or loans against his future expenses from the company petty cash float. He was now in a quandary. He was tempted to ambush the Export Manager at the next executive committee, but felt that, apart from the fact that it was not how he preferred to manage situations, the matter could destroy the credibility of the Export Manager, which might not be in the best interests of the company which at the time needed all the export sales it could gain. In addition, it would hardly be a good advertisement for the company's own internal controls.

Rather than launch an ambush, which might also have been seen by colleagues as revenge-motivated and thus somewhat discredited, the discovery was simply made known to the Chairman who took stringent but confidential action.

———— KEY TECHNIQUE ————

Those who plan and use ambushes must be prepared to defend themselves against subsequent 'revenge' attacks. Indeed, it could be argued as a golden rule that only those who are absolutely sure of their own position and are 'squeaky clean' should mount such attacks.

Corporate ambush

Whilst many ambushes occur wholly within an organisation, in the corporate field, which has been, perhaps more accurately, described as a jungle being populated by those more akin to wild beasts than humans, such ambushes are far from rare. Operating from this arena rather than internally is, however, no guarantee of success, particularly if the perpetrators lose sight of the 'absolute security' golden rule.

CASE STUDY 11.2 **Double whammy**

The Managing Director had been headhunted by a merchant banker to run a company, which under its previous Managing Director had lost its way, got into difficulties, and was now trying to recover. The arrangement was that the previous Managing Director would become non-executive Chairman for six months prior to leaving the company altogether. This would clear the way for the newcomer. Although trading losses were being incurred, capital was not a problem as the merchant banker had introduced a venture capitalist to the company, whose nominee had joined the Board. Soon after taking up his position, it became clear to the newcomer that his predecessor had no real intention of relinquishing his executive role, or ultimately of leaving the company. His reaction when the subject was broached was to delay things 'until the trading position improved'. The difficulty was that the Chairman, who had been largely responsible for the deterioration of the trading position, was still interfering in such activities and worsening the position.

Matters came to a head at a Board meeting when the Chairman's anger at his potential sidelining overflowed into open aggression, and it became clear that there was an irreconcilable personality clash between the two men. Subsequently two additional Directors were appointed who, it soon became clear, sided with the Chairman rather than the new Managing Director. This led to conflict within the Board in which the new Managing Director was invariably the loser. Eventually a Board meeting was convened at which the question of the Chairman leaving the company was raised, only for the meeting to be told that he had changed his mind and would stay for at least a further month during which period a further Board meeting was convened.

▶

▶

At that meeting, without any prior indication, the Chairman proposed a vote of no-confidence in the new Managing Director which, with support from the two new Directors, was passed by a majority vote. Accordingly, the new Managing Director was asked to go.

Fortunately for him, the company had institutional shareholders who had been reassured by his appointment following the search by the merchant banker, and, on them investigating the situation, the ambush was negated and the shareholders demanded and got the new MD's reinstatement, followed by the resignation of all the ambushing opposition.

———— KEY TECHNIQUE ————

Intervention by shareholders or owners in this fashion is rare although many institutional shareholders are becoming more aware of the need for them to take action in certain circumstances, and recent research disclosed that the numbers of such shareholders prepared to vote on corporate matters had increased by over 60 per cent in a year.

Defences

Since ambushes are by definition unexpected, it is difficult to prepare for them other than by trying at all times to appreciate the lie of power within a meeting. Whilst power in a meeting may shift depending on the subject matter under discussion, most perceptive members will soon realise that there are usually two or three key members whose views tend to sway discussions and decisions. Without any formal alliance with such members, an appreciation of one's standing with them might help an overall appreciation of the chance of survival in the event of an ambush being mounted.

In the first fifteen months of the UK's Conservative Government elected in 1992, no less than three cabinet members were forced to go, in situations that were less than clear-cut. It is arguable that, ignoring the poor judgement exercised in each case, what ultimately brought about their termination, was a lack of a power base in their own party. Other persons of similar status, commanding, or being able to rely on, a substantial following in the party, might well have been able to survive.

Such lack of a power base compounded by the loss of confidence from one's colleagues is the ultimate ambush. This automatically suggests that we need to check our alliances and allies carefully so that we know when to use them

---

CASE STUDY 11.3 **Quick thinking**

The Finance Director, promoted from another company to his present position and determined to make his mark regardless of other executives, was well known for mini ambushes at executive meetings. On one occasion, following the presentation of the departmental report from the personnel function, he baldly stated that there was no need for the additional labour suggested; what was required was for the existing personnel to be better trained and he could not understand why training schemes were not already in operation.

'Oh but they are,' replied the Personnel Director, kicking the Production Director under the table quietly, 'We've developed a comprehensive product knowledge/ awareness programme and I am finalising it with Joe. Is that not right Joe?'

'Absolutely' replied the Production Director on cue, delighted, having suffered from the Finance Director's ambushes before, to be able to wrong-foot him.

'Why isn't it in your report then?' snapped the Finance Director, furious that it seemed his prey was escaping.

'Because, before we implement it, we need to put up a capital expenditure application, in accordance with your requirements, as it will need some equipment and materials. You should have the application within 48 hours but we do need a prompt decision. As you are obviously very keen on the idea as well, presumably that should be no problem, should it?'

KEY TECHNIQUE

The Finance Director had experienced the tables being turned on him, to the quiet delight of most other meeting members. In addition, he had a reputation for unnecessarily delaying and querying capital expenditure forms. As, at the meeting, he had gone on record stating how necessary the training was he could hardly then hold up the application when it was submitted.

Postponements and adjournments

Faced with an ambush, few people may be able to think swiftly enough, as did the Personnel and Production Directors in Case Study 11.3. Points of order may then be the only defence, for example:

- question if the item being raised is within the aegis of the meeting itself. If not it should be ignored;

- make some apparently convincing reply, as in Case Sudy 11.3 or 'that's a very good point and something that has been troubling me for some time, so much so that I have been trying to gather together a few facts for a short report which I was hoping to present to the committee at its next meeting';

- request an adjournment whilst the finer detail of the point is investigated. This has the advantage of inferring that the main thrust of the question had already been considered prior to it being raised at the meeting and a detailed report on the matter is in course of preparation;

- request a recess to check details with the department;

- feign illness!

CASE STUDY 11.4   Team in disharmony

The subsidiary Managing Director was leading the wage negotiations assisted by the group Personnel Executive. After considerable discussion the Managing Director stated that the company would accept the union's revised pay demand. Since this was diametrically opposed to his instructions the Group Executive was stunned and swiftly developed a coughing fit to the point of near fainting, which threw the meeting into confusion. He asked for a glass of water and when it was brought coughed so much when he started to sip it that it was spilled. As a result two or three of the meeting members left the room for some time, during which hiatus the Personnel Executive was able to whisper to the Managing Director that the suggestion of agreement would break the group's policy on wage increases and would raise all kinds of issues regarding differentials. He requested the Director to phone the Group Chairman before proceeding. Whilst the latter left the office to make the call the Personnel Executive gradually 'recovered'.

Loss of confidence = assassination

Sometimes the ambush may appear a more leisurely affair, particularly where it is a question of a growing unease with performance. In this case few of the defences may be appropriate which may make its use in this way more effective.

CASE STUDY 11.5   **The friendly assassins**

After a fruitless search for a new divisional Chief Executive, including being turned down by two selected candidates, the company ultimately decided to appoint a person who had scored highly but had been no one's ideal choice. Unfortunately, although every effort was made to support and help him, it swiftly became clear that he was not the right person for the job, and although at each meeting the requirements for action were laid down clearly, he was unable to rise to the challenge.

The Chairman and a Senior Director discussed the problem.

'The trouble is that every meeting is becoming increasingly embarrassing which is doing great harm to the relationship between him and his colleagues as they see that he cannot cope.'

'I try to support him at every instance.'

▶

> 'I know but the problem with that is what you are doing is plain for all to see. The situation is not good for the business, not good for the team and in reality, it's not good for him.'
>
> 'Then let's have it out with him at the next meeting.'
>
> 'That's the worst thing to do. We must see him privately, see how he feels things are going and if he does not agree that things cannot continue as they are, then we shall have to suggest that he resigns. At least that way we won't have a potentially damaging and embarrassing row in meeting.'
>
> 'You mean try to save his face.'
>
> 'Yes, but not just his face, ours as well. After all we appointed him, it was our decision.'
>
> The problem was discussed with the Chief Executive, who, whilst not agreeing that things were as out-of-control as his colleagues obviously felt, was not happy with the situation and agreed to resign as he had lost the confidence of his colleagues.

_____ KEY TECHNIQUE _____

There was nothing to be gained, and much to be lost, by generating an open row in meeting; friendliness could win the day and achieve the same aims. The Board had manipulated the position to the ends that they had determined were those required by the company, and in the process assassinated (in a business sense) a fellow executive.

Testing support

In Case Study 11.5, it seemed to those involved that the position must be clear already to the Chief Executive. However, whilst he was aware that things were not as good as they could be and his performance was not rated highly, he had no idea that his colleagues found the position so alarming and urgent. Yet his predecessor, who had run the division very successfully for several years, was still with the organisation and available for consultation and advice. The problem was related more to the newcomer's belief in his own capacity to deal with the problems and opportunities and his apparent unwillingness to, or unawareness of the value of, testing out his ideas on his colleagues. The rationale of testing ideas is not just to obtain other views and suggestions, but also to test support. After all, if the Chief Executive had regularly checked out the reactions of the Senior Director or the Chairman, he would have soon discovered, informally, their very real concern, and might have been able to rectify the situation prior to it deteriorating beyond recovery. Apart from any other considerations, testing reactions and ideas with other meeting members is flattering to most people and tends to generate mutual support, may generate ideas which they can support (as they will claim some credit for such ideas) and can provide enlightenment as to the views of one's colleagues.

The purpose of testing support is to generate reactions and gain insight into others' views. Whilst this is usually to garner information to aid the preparation and promulgation of a case, equally it may disclose information or indicate opposition likely against a pet project. In this, it is not so much what people may say as what they do not say which can be revealing. This is reminiscent of the comment said to have been made by a past adversary when he learned of the death of the arch manipulator and arranger, Metternich: 'I wonder what he meant by that'.

CASE STUDY 11.6 **Read my mind not my words**

The meeting of the Directors was informal to discuss the question of the succession and composition of the Board. The claims of a number of contenders for Board appointments were discussed as well as the potential balance of the Board after implementation of the changes. In discussing the conclusions in private subsequently one Director was considerably taken aback when his colleague questioned whether he really thought the Deputy Chairman would take over from the Chairman on the latter's retirement. This had been assumed, and had been taken for granted at the meeting, although no decision had been taken by the Deputy Chairman at the time. The observant Director pointed out that at no time during the conversation, had the Deputy Chairman stated how he wished to see the Board, but had been content for the present Chairman to state his own conjectures.

─────── KEY TECHNIQUE ───────

Sometimes we can learn as much from what is not said as from what is said. Listening carefully may gain a greater edge than propounding one's own case.

This parallels Mandy Rice-Davies' classic comment when asked her view of words uttered by another, 'Well, he would say that, wouldn't he'. Not only was her reply stating the obvious, but also it correctly implied that the question originally posed which brought about the answer was pretty pointless since the answer it would generate was obvious. Further, despite the question being asked, one would still not know whether truth had been disclosed. If a man on trial for murder is asked, 'have you ever murdered anyone?' he is hardly likely to reply 'yes', so the question is pointless. The answer given may be either true or false and one will not necessarily know which – the possibility of being prosecuted for perjury is hardly a worry to the guilty.

Sometimes simple silence, or a lack of comment, can indicate the lie of our thoughts to the perceptive questioner, and equally such silence can be used by a perceptive person to bluff an inquisitor. All that is needed is an appreciation of what a person would say if their thoughts were running in a particular way. One then needs to frame an answer which seems to be the type of comment that would be made in such circumstances and to deliver it with the kind of conviction that would be applicable in that situation.

Manipulating realities

The problem with this kind of thought manipulation is that it depends on others seeing things in the same way as we do. We may be very unwise to base a particular course of action on the assumption that if we tell A a fact, he is sure to tell B and C, because that is what we would do in his position. We may then take certain action, being sure that B and C will understand because A must have told them, only to fail when, against all expectations, A keeps the item to himself and B and C remain entirely in the dark. Rumour manipulation in this way can be very effective, rather like flying a kite to gauge reaction, but may be totally useless if the rumour does not spread to the target required, or is used too often, or is simply not believed. In the light of losses to the Exchequer, caused partly by the UK recession of the early 1990s, the Government needed to examine its spending. In the course of what was, presumably, a confidential review, several rumours of proposed cuts in social spending were floated into the public arena, in order it seemed, to test reaction and to create a pecking order dependent upon how much outrage was provoked.

Scandalmongers

Rumour is often depicted as multi-headed. Like the Hydra of Greek mythology it is also supposed to grow more 'heads' should one be cut off or eliminated. It can also be likened to weeds – quick to grow and difficult to eradicate. Some people are able to manipulate their colleagues and the meeting simply by creating or fostering rumours. This can be achieved either by the active method of contributing to the rumour and ensuring that it is passed on, or the passive method of simply raising doubts which create a question mark over the project in the minds of other members.

CASE STUDY 11.7   **'Someone told a friend, who told me ...'**

The Director was very much against a new proposal that the company should branch out into a related but separate field of operation, but realised that most of his colleagues were in favour of the suggestion. When the recommendation came to be discussed, at a late stage in the debate, he commented: 'I had heard that X [a competitor who had been operating for about a year in a similar field of operations] had made very little money from the product and was thinking of pulling out of the concept'. Whether the statement had any validity or not, and checking the true position might be difficult or impossible, and would certainly take time, the meeting came to a sudden halt. The Director had achieved his aim without any facts at his disposal.

——— KEY TECHNIQUE ———

Obviously were such a device used repeatedly it would, unless there actually were facts to back it up, destroy the perpetrator's reputation. The counter might be for the Chairman to rule that such comments should only be made if facts were there to back the statement, but this is dangerous as sometimes a rumour does have validity. Indeed, the problem with rumours, and particularly in defeating or denying them, is that often they do contain a kernel of truth.

The other trick of the scandalmonger is to throw doubt on the capability of a person involved in the project. 'Oh I had heard that XYZ Ltd were not impressed with the work he did for them on their project.' Once again, without any facts to support it, a niggling doubt has been placed in the minds of the supporters of the project that they might have the wrong man for the job. This kind of action, when totally baseless, is scandalous and is probably also actionable. However, it is effective and can be difficult to combat, although, if used repeatedly, it will lose its effectiveness, as it will if the 'whisper' can be successfully challenged.

CASE STUDY 11.8   **Collapse of stout party**

The Board was discussing a proposed joint venture agreement to which the Sales Director was very antipathetic, as the other party was a competitor. The technical expertise would be contributed by the competitor whereas the marketing would be carried out in-house, whilst, to protect both parties, actual production would be bought in from a third party. The Sales Director commented that he understood 'from the trade', a source which it was virtually impossible to check, that the technical expertise available was currently being questioned and was likely to be replaced by the competitor company. The Chairman, suspecting the committee was being conned by false evidence, bluffed in his turn by commenting that he was lunching with the Chairman of the competitor the following day and would enquire. The Sales Director, aware that his reputation might be damaged when the story was found to be false, back-pedalled furiously, pointing out that (a) it was only a rumour, (b) currently the trade 'was full of rumours at present', and (c) obviously many such rumours would be false and perhaps therefore it would be unwise to rely on such a rumour without checking its accuracy.

CHAPTER TWELVE

Snowballs and deserts

Key learning points

- If data is tabled for instant decision the fact should be noted in the minutes

- If the above situation is repeated a formal objection may be advisable

- If data is not available, or is stated to have 'gone astray', the fact should be noted in the minutes

- Constant repetition of or reference to a previous 'underhand' device may force a compensatory move

Snowballing

The need for data to be sent out with the agenda at least a week before the meeting was made earlier. Despite this rule there will be occasions when data has to be sent out just before the meeting or even tabled at the meeting, and where circumstances dictate, this may need to be accepted. However, the 'lateness of availability' excuse is a valuable one which can be used by the unscrupulous to attempt manipulation. In this event, what may be complex data, requiring quiet study and assimilation is simply tabled at the meeting and members have no opportunity to study it. They may then need to rely on a synopsis presented verbally by the perpetrator. This can be compounded by the perpetrator, having held back the data, requiring an instantaneous decision to achieve a particular timetable. Effectively, the perpetrator is extorting the meeting's instant acceptance, and gaining its combined authority and responsibility for the proposal.

CASE STUDY 12.1   **Vote please**

On attending a committee meeting, the organisation's appointee was disconcerted to find tabled a complex report regarding the possible investment of a substantial sum of the Federation's assets. The recommendation was contained in a closely-typed 60-page report and a decision was required immediately to take advantage of a 'window of opportunity'.

Since there was no way the import of the report could be obtained whilst the meeting was in session, the appointee suggested that the committee take a 45 minute break whilst members reviewed the report and had an opportunity to question the author. This was agreed even though the time available was totally inadequate for the purpose.

──────── KEY TECHNIQUE ────────

In agreeing to the recommendation, the appointee stipulated that the minutes of the meeting should show that the members, other than the perpetrator and his allies, had only had a restricted time to consider the proposal and stated that if such a situation repeated itself he would vote against such a piece of business on principle.

Control of snowballing

Whilst, in some cases, there may be no alternative to consideration of such an item submitted late, it may be advisable to stipulate the rules covering such an eventuality (*see* Fig. 12.1).

1 Decisions on matters (other than purely routine items) tabled at a meeting should not be expected other than in instances of extreme urgency concerning the determination of which the decision of the Chairman will be final.

2 Any member tabling a report must provide a one-page guide to the salient points, with a recommendation for action and an explanation of the reason for the delay.

3 Such a summary must include both advantages and disadvantages backing and/or leading to the proposal.

4 The summary must be confirmed (by being signed) as fair and accurate by at least one director.

5 Although the decision in principle may be taken at the meeting, absolute commitment will not be granted for 48 hours after the meeting to allow members time for quiet reconsideration.

Figure 12.1   Guidelines to control snowballing

Deliberate complexity

Complex language and a mass of data tend to repel most readers. The requirement for a one-page summary may do much to rectify this. Standards of literacy and numeracy are not high in the United Kingdom, and recent research indicates that even though we have used a decimal currency for over 28 years, 47 per cent of the population experience difficulty with percentages. Sadly the authors of many documents ignore the interests of their target audience, either accidentally through not appreciating their problems, or even deliberately in order either to preserve their own status or to ensure the real messages being conveyed do not get through to provoke any reaction. The mass of the data confuses and obscures the essential messages. For example, the Institute of Chartered Accountants of Scotland states in its book *Making Corporate Reports Valuable* that 'present-day financial statements are often almost incomprehensible to anyone other than their preparers'. Yet financial statements are essential documents that must be provided for all the joint owners of a company to make certain decisions based on the items contained in the report.

Research carried out by MORI indicates that only about 20 per cent of those who receive such reports read some or all of the report, whilst further research indicates that only about 75 per cent of them claim to understand them and only 33 per cent of *them*, when tested, actually do have a reasonable understanding of the content. Thirty-three per cent of 75 per cent of 20 per cent is ... a very low number! Whilst sympathising with those who have to grapple with the presentation of statutory requirements, it does seem that often too little is done to present the data in a form where it is capable of being understood by its target audience. This is hardly a sound basis for the decisions which must be taken upon it. In recognition of this problem corporate reporting rules have been relaxed so that companies are now allowed to send simplified financial statements in place of the full report. Where these have been produced they do seem to be user-friendly, and can thus provide the information needed. Of course, it would be preferable to make the original report actually perform the communication role for which they were intended.

When designing reports it is sometimes overlooked that the report will be compared to other examples of reading material – whether these be newspapers, journals or magazines. The manner in which the messages are conveyed in these publications, and the effect they have on the way in which the reader then expects to receive other written information, should not be underestimated. The impact of mass media has conditioned us to look for certain information 'trails' and, therefore, to become confused if there is either an absence of such a trail, or if the layout is one with which we are not familiar. A statement or report needs to be presented in a way that both invites the reader to start and is easily followed through.[1]

Deserts

At least the consolation with snowballing and being subjected to information via complex material is that, despite the pressure to make a decision, one does actually have available all the information on which a decision can be based. The problem is one of assimilation and comprehension, to allow understanding to generate a decision. The converse of being snowballed at a meeting is finding oneself bereft of all data, literally in a data desert. One is then being forced to make a contrived decision without data being available.

---

[1] (from the author's book *How To Prepare the Annual Report*, Institute of Directors, 1989)

CASE STUDY 12.2   **Take it all on trust**

In Case Study 10.4, the Board believed the Managing Director was competent to take the company forward, however he had no record with the company on which his colleagues could build any trust. In presenting the Board with a plan, his colleagues pointed out that they could hardly agree it since it consisted of virtually baseless projections, whilst a marketing strategy, cash flow projections and balance sheet were all missing. Effectively the Board was being asked to approve and grant support to the Managing Director's view of the future, and to rely entirely on his 'gut feeling' as 'time had not allowed' the preparation of the other matters.

———— KEY TECHNIQUE ————

In fact the Board agreed to approve the plan but only in outline and purely to enable the Managing Director to talk to the company's bankers to gain their support.

Making a decision without sufficient information can be the mark of a brilliant entrepreneur and is usually publicised as such. Such brilliance (or luck) tends to be a rare exception of course and little is heard of the decisions which failed. In general the rule should be that before making a decision at a meeting members need information. Starving them of such information may be enough to force them into agreeing a decision once, but it is hardly likely that a repeat performance will be allowed. Once again the tactic of requiring the minutes to show that the decision had to be made without back-up data and on the recommendation of the [named] member may ensure such a blackmailing move is not repeated.

Gone astray

Inferring that information, properly and timely sent, has gone astray is a particularly nasty variation of the contrived desert tactic, as it is essentially believable, although it becomes less so if repeated. It is very difficult to prove, even if one is personally convinced, that the papers were never actually sent. The result is that alone amongst one's colleagues you may not have the data on which a decision is needed. There is little point in referring to the Chairman's rules (Fig. 12.1) as other members' copies have found their true destinations. Even requiring a note in the minutes can backfire as underlying the whole can be an inference that the documents were correctly sent, correctly received and their non-appearance is one's own responsibility. Obviously the device can only be used rarely and one way of combating it, if a colleague is suspected of deliberately starving one of information, is to stipulate that you wish to collect the data.

Bigmouths

The principle of a bigmouth's operation is to shout very loud and long to enhance reputation but to avoid actually doing anything. Such people can usually talk very convincingly and knowledgeably, making a cogent case and arguing forcefully against any adverse comments. But when it comes to obtaining action, however, they slide away from the commitment, often claiming to be so committed already that they cannot contribute to the implementation of the project despite this enthusiasm for it. Rather like the bully, their presence, if they generate good ideas, may be tolerated, despite the lack of implementation preparedness. However, the reaction of their colleagues should be tested, since if they feel aggrieved that they are left to implement ideas put forward by the bigmouth, then the Chairman may need to put the latter's commitment on the line. This will entail asking them to implement their own ideas. Should such a commitment be lacking, a declaration that, in that case, the project should not proceed, may be the ultimate test. The bigmouth is told that it's 'put up or shut up' time.

Meetings, however, do tend to draw unequal contributions from their members. Unless care is taken, and members' contributions are regularly assessed, it is possible for some members to 'hide amongst the trees' and for their lack of contribution to be compensated by others. This is usually acceptable to other members if the 'quiet member' is also an action contributor, that is he or she actually performs outside the meeting in order to help the meeting meet its aims. Conversely irritation and consid-erable demotivation, can be caused by non-performing 'bigmouths'.

CASE STUDY 12.3   **Talks a lot – does very little**

Ted, a committee member, was becoming irritated by Bill, another member, as, although Bill seemed able to catch the Chairman's eye when comments were invited and to hold the floor and have a great deal to say about most subjects, it was clear to him, though not it seemed to others, that in terms of actually doing anything, Bill was always able to slide away and evade responsibility. He sounded out Sue, another member, and found that she agreed.

At the next meeting when Bill commented on a particular item of business, Ted agreed that his comments were apposite and that he should be asked to carry out the idea. Bill demurred, pleading lack of time. This was repeated twice in the same meeting, each time Bill having to state publicly that he could not undertake the work. At the end of the meeting, Sue asked the Secretary if he could check through who was doing what. Ted interrupted this run through to comment, 'Surely that was Bill's idea and he is doing it, isn't he?' Bill was forced to repeat that he wasn't.

At the end of the following meeting when the same tactics were repeated, Ted idly asked Bill if he did not mind that all his suggestions were being followed up by others.

———— KEY TECHNIQUE ————

This neatly brought the matter to the attention of the Chairman who, having been made aware both of the situation and of the attitude of others on the committee, suggested to Bill that either he become accountable or he leave the committee.

The circumstances of the situation outlined in Case Study 12.3 encouraged action from the other members as action was expected from all members. This may not be the case in all meetings and in some situations it would be quite acceptable for there to be in the meeting members without responsibility for implementing ideas; indeed, this is part of the principle behind the appointment of Non-executive Directors to Boards of Directors of public listed companies in the United Kingdom. They can bring extra experience and knowledge to the Board, make suggestions and give advice and yet have no executive responsibility for implementation.

Buzzers

A derivative of the 'bigmouth' is the 'buzzer' who, like his mentor, talks volubly and knowledgeably. However, the buzzer lards his talk with buzz words and phrases which sound very authoritative and learned and yet, if challenged or examined, can be seen to be trite and shallow. The aim of the buzzer is to create an impression of being completely 'au fait' with the subject matter even though this may not be the case. The phrase implies the speaker knows exactly what he is talking about and that it is entirely relevant to the discussion, whereas often neither may be true.

CASE STUDY 12.4 **Baffling the listener**

The discussion at the meeting concerned the choice of music to be included in the end of term concert. The suggestions included works by Handel and Mozart. After some heated discussion, one member attempted to close off the conversation and dismiss the inclusion of the two items with the phrase 'of course these works by Handel and Mozart are inadequate intellectually'. This fine sounding phrase stopped all discussion, as other members hesitantly agreed. The inclusion of the works was dropped until some time later another member, having had time to consider the phrase, pointed out that what was wanted was a balanced musical programme and that no one had even claimed that the music should be adequate intellectually – it was not relevant. Indeed, neither Handel nor Mozart intended their work to be intellectual – they wrote to entertain as wide an audience as possible.

──────── KEY TECHNIQUE ────────

One should not be afraid, when faced with convincing sounding arguments to state, 'I am sorry I do not understand your point. Could you please explain what you mean?'

Triteness

Similarly, the use of trite phrases in the middle of a meeting can cause a hiatus, divert discussion and sometimes act almost as a dismissal of the subject without any explanation of the meaning behind the phrase being required.

CASE STUDY 12.5   **Too trite**

The in-house presentation had concluded and a meeting was being held with delegates to assess its value for repetition elsewhere. One member, who had attended under protest, dismissed the presentation as 'all chalk and talk'. Since one or two other delegates agreed, the Personnel Manager, who had not been on the course, was concerned and wondered if he should source alternative presenters. Before doing so he decided to check the content and found that, far from the dismissive phrase used, delegates had been involved in discussions, had a chance to comment on hand-outs, worked through case studies and been involved in syndicate exercises.

————— KEY TECHNIQUE —————

The damage of phrases like this is that they create an immediate and lasting impression which is in part bound to be correct since 'talk and chalk' is inherent in virtually all presentations. However, the comment is shallow and misleading, and its alliteration contributes to its dismissiveness and creates an impression out of all proportion to its value. To rebuff such comments is essential. Even a swift challenge such as 'I think that is rather a shallow comment in view of ...' may place the commentator on the defensive.

Misleading data

Whilst it is rare that members are actually misled by their colleagues, the rarity of its incidence indicates a need for meeting members to be on their guard against such a device.

CASE STUDY 12.6   **Never mind the figures, feel the quality**

The investors were bemused by the figures presented to them by the Managing Director of the company in which they had invested. In view of the recession and the fact that the company had been subjected to considerable competition, they found the projection for the full year's figures very encouraging.

'We're hoping to convince a number of shareholders to put up some more capital,' said the Managing Director. 'In that way we will be able to press on with the upgrading of some of the factory equipment.'

'I can't understand how it is that these figures are so much better than the previous estimates,' said one investor.

'Well we did have a very good August,' said the Managing Director.

'It may have been good but you were still well below budget for the month,' said the other investor. 'You've removed the first two months' loss-making trading from these figures. The cumulative sales and profit figures you are showing only cover the last six months of the year!'

———— KEY TECHNIQUE ————

Ensure all data is prepared with adequate controls and presented complete in every respect.

First the good news

Whereas most manipulation occurs within a factual context, it is possible for some to occur within a timeframe. Decisions can only be taken on the basis of data known and if the data is unknown, as in the example of the desert, then the meeting may need to guess. However, in some cases a decision is avoided or delayed merely because the meeting is unaware of the need for one to be taken, as it has been manipulated by one of its members usurping its authority and decision-making process.

CASE STUDY 12.7   **Playing poker**

The results for the year were likely to be poor but could be rescued to some extent by the sale of properties. Just before the meeting, however, the Property Director was told by the company's agents that the purchasers of two properties had withdrawn from the deals, which meant that the enhancing of the results by the property transactions was imperilled. The Director stressed to the agents that he needed new deals concluded as quickly as possible but concealed the failure of the current two from the meeting. By the time of the following meeting the two new deals were in place.

———— KEY TECHNIQUE ————

It is arguable that no harm was done in the circumstances set out in Case Study 12.7, although of course the Director concealed a material fact from the Board and had the replacement deals not been found he, as well as the Board and the company, could have been seriously embarrassed. To avoid such temptation the Chairman needs to stress that the meeting needs to know everything at all times, whether it be good or bad, and whilst culpability may not be an issue regarding events outside members' control, suppression of information (or actually misleading the Board of the true state of the situation, as here) cannot be tolerated.

Absentees

So far this chapter has concentrated on the activities of members trying to sway the meeting by their own presence and the absence or presence of data. However, some members can have a considerable affect on the meeting by their personal absence. Thus the first investor in Case Study 12.5 had good reason to be thankful his colleague was present, as had his colleague not spotted the deception, he might have invested further. Instigators of business should check the attendance intentions of members in advance. Directors have obligations to attend meetings of the Board of limited companies to the point of being removed from office if they miss meetings over a six-month period without good cause. This precedent of required attendance may apply to other meetings.

What is required at a meeting is the attendance and attention of precisely those, but only those, necessary to enable the business to be conducted. Absence of a key contributor can destroy the effectiveness of the meeting and thus, should this be anticipated, either the meeting may need to be postponed, or in some way the views of the missing member need to be relayed to the meeting. Whether proxies or alternates are allowed to attend the meeting instead of the missing member will depend on its terms of reference. If proxies are allowed, then it is essential that the exact views of the absentee are represented accurately by the proxy. This may mean he needs to refer back to his principal, or that the principal's instructions are reduced to written notes for the proxy's guidance, or that a third party witnesses the briefing and is available to corroborate the proxy's statements if necessary, and so avoid misrepresentation.

Where proxies or alternates are not permissible, then the views of the missing member need to be canvassed, possibly by the Chairman, or, should there be a possibility of the Chairman and the member holding opposing views, by a person who agrees with the views of the missing member, in order to avoid misrepresentation. Obviously where a key member of the meeting is absent, only those matters on the agenda, and those items on which it has been possible to gain his/her views, should be discussed. The Chairman may need to intervene if, seizing the opportunity of the member's absence, other members try to push through business which it is known the missing member opposes.

Review

Circumventing the machinations of those who seek to divert the meeting and/or its business to their own ends will aid the progress of the meeting to its aims on the basis of Macbeth's advice, 'if it were done when 'tis done, then 'twere well it were done quickly'. The speed with which business is conducted in meetings is not necessarily indicative of effectiveness. However, preparedness for such devices will concentrate the attention of the members on the salient points which should, in turn, benefit effectiveness. There is an ongoing need for the effectiveness of the meeting to be considered regularly to check if it is attaining its aims or not, and if not, how arrangements can be improved to ensure that it does. Perhaps it is inevitable that members should disagree on this point but, if the question is posed regularly, it should:

- remind members that the meeting should have 'meat' and point out what its aims are

- challenge them to consider their own effectiveness individually, as well as that of the meeting as a whole

- encourage objective consideration of the attainments of the meeting since the previous assessment.

In carrying out such an assessment, the Chairman may need to convene a meeting, to which all the guidance regarding pitfalls and problems already set out also apply. If, as Alexander Pope stated, 'the proper study of mankind is man,' then the proper study and understanding of meetings is the study of the members of the meeting, some of whom may not take kindly to the suggestion. Had such ongoing assessment been carried out then the committee in Case Study 1.1 would have very quickly realised that its existence, other than for the social end, had become redundant.

CASE STUDY 12.8   **The unproductive productivity scheme committee**

The committee had been set up to implement the company's productivity reward scheme which had been running for a year. As part of its terms of reference, it was required to set up individual departmental working parties which could take forward productivity improvement ideas and concepts. At each meeting these ideas and concepts were considered and queries and questions resolved. Whilst originally a considerable amount of time was spent generating the working parties and dealing with the questions, these eventually tailed off and the committee's work degenerated into reading the previous meeting's minutes, noting the actions of the working parties and setting the date of its next meeting. Eventually the Secretary pointed out that the greatest lack of productivity left in the company was the time spent in the steering committee meetings and it was immediately agreed to cease meeting except when one of the departmental groups had a problem.

Assessing the members

As well as the members assessing how effective their contributions have been, the Chairman may also need to assess the contribution of the various members. Certainly, if the members have been using some of the devices described in this and the previous four chapters then perhaps their continued membership of the meeting should be reconsidered. After all, to be effective a meeting needs effective members. Members who need to resort to destructive, manipulative devices are hardly likely to be effective meeting members.

CHAPTER THIRTEEN

Meet the media

Key learning points

■ Cultivating media contacts should ensure more accurate and possibly sympathetic reporting

■ Those briefing the media, need to be adequately briefed and trained

■ Comprehensive guidelines need to be produced, adhered to and regularly updated to aid such a briefing process

Public interest

The operations and activities of companies are increasingly subject to the attention of 'the media', either as stories in their own right, or as part of a larger, and possibly investigative, 'story'. Whilst the incidence of such attention is greater for companies which are 'household names', or whose products or services which are well-known and/or controversial (since attention can arise and/or increase dramatically when a crisis in the operation occurs), all organisations should make some preparations for contacts and media meetings. Reputation and public awareness may be indefinable and incapable of quantification, nevertheless their value can be considerable. A reputation which took years to build can be lost in a few seconds. The company that has not prepared for this, that has not cultivated media contacts or has not rehearsed for the investigative or even hostile approach may find it virtually impossible to counter adverse comment, or to promulgate its own version of events.

Since 'good' news stories tend not to capture or stir the readers' attention as much as 'bad', the latter stories tend to dominate reporting. Thus there tends to be:

a) a requirement to concentrate on 'what went wrong' to the exclusion of 'what is going right' and

b) a need for instant updating of news items which, by virtue of the speed of transmission, lends itself to mistakes ranging from a straightforward misinterpretation to deliberate falsification.

This pressure to deliver copy must be recognised and allowed for. Organisations should make and cultivate suitable contacts, brief them regularly on developments and happenings, and encourage them to ask questions. Setting up this kind of programme will enable the organisation to foster contacts that *understand* the business. When newsworthy stories break, a person asked to write a story without such knowledge may be under considerable pressure to guess facts and conclusions. Misunderstandings tend to occur resulting in an ill-informed story. Conversely, 'in touch' and ongoing contacts in the media, by virtue of their ingrained knowledge of the organisation and of its people and products, will have a far more informed insight and be able to report more objectively and knowledgeably, and possibly more sympathetically about the organisation than would otherwise be the case.

A comprehensive approach incorporating policy, research, crisis reaction, training and practice is essential. A suitable policy and/or procedure should be adopted (*see* Fig. 13.1).

General

1 The organisation recognises the natural interest that will be evinced by the media in its operations and will make all information, other than that which is regarded as confidential, regularly available.

2 [Name and deputy] will act as spokesperson for the organisation and will be briefed continually by those responsible for each [division, product, etc.].

3 In the event of other employees being contacted by media representatives, they will always be referred to the spokesperson.

4 In interfacing with the media, the spokesperson will endeavour to be truthful at all times, and to ensure that such information is correctly reported.

Figure 13.1   Draft media communication policy

5 All media contacts will be regularly briefed so that they have background knowledge of the organisation, updated continuously.

6 In the event of a serious occurrence the senior manager responsible must brief the spokesperson as quickly as possible so that he or she, in turn, is ready to answer media questions.

Research

No briefing or interview will be successful unless adequate preparation and research has been carried out. Thus the following are necessary:

1 Identify the areas of operation in which the media could be interested.

2 Identify the target audiences and the information they will be seeking.

3 Establish who is to deal with the ongoing enquiry and how they are to be briefed and updated concerning progress and all related aspects.

4 Encourage the spokesperson to create links with media representatives, establishing names, positions, main interests or 'angles', deadlines, bias, and so on.

5 Examine all stories and reports concerning the organisation and its products to ensure that the correct image is being created, attempting to use the contacts to correct false impressions.

6 Continually develop questions, and answers thereto, that the company least wants asked and become conversant with both, updated as necessary.

7 Prepare and update a résumé of all the successes of the company so that good news is available to leaven the bad.

Crisis reaction

Whilst briefing the media on the more mundane aspects of company performance may be relatively easy, dealing with such interest in the aftermath of a calamity or disaster poses considerable problems which are capable of being tackled only if based on contingency planning, that is anticipating the disaster and making advance plans for dealing with anticipated effects. The advantage of 'planning for disaster' is that lengthy and calm thought can be given to alternative tactics and reactions, without the considerable pressure that the incidence of disaster can cause. In addition, consideration of alternative actions in the event of disaster, may suggest beneficial changes in current operations. Obviously, if it is to be of value, such planning must be both comprehensive and regularly updated.

Figure 13.1   Continued

> **Checklist: crisis reaction**
>
> **1** Initial contact will usually be by telephone. A person should be nominated, possibly the Company Secretary, though there should always be one or two back-up personnel to handle initial queries if the spokesperson is not available.
>
> **2** Keep calm and listen to what the enquirer is asking.
>
> **3** Make notes of (or tape) the call content, time, the caller's name, position and media represented, the caller's telephone number and location.
>
> **4** Do *not* respond to questions, comments, observations – simply make notes as set out in 3 above and state that by a (stated) time someone will respond either in a press release or by telephone, and so on.
>
> **5** Do *not* be flustered by indications of deadlines, insistence on immediate response, outrageous accusations, or innuendo.
>
> **6** By the time promised, not less than an hour, ensure that someone does call the enquirer back with comments.
>
> **7** Keep responses, press statements, and so on, short. Embroidery can both offset the punch effect and provide other 'angles' from which the reporter can come back at the author.
>
> **8** Provide a contact name/number.
>
> **9** Should such contact be used then the above guidelines should be applied. If necessary the spokesperson should ring back after time for thought.
>
> **10** If press releases are used, these need to be drafted carefully so that:
>
>   **a)** the essential features of the news to be reported are contained in the first paragraph
>
>   **b)** the news must be of substance and presented concisely and clearly
>
>   **c)** it provides usable quotes from named authorities
>
>   **d)** it specifies a realistic release date and gives an in-house contact and telephone number.

Figure 13.1   Continued

Training the spokesperson

The spokesperson needs considerable personal knowledge of the organisation which can be augmented by detailed input from time to time by those personally responsible. However, such background briefing, whilst essential, is not sufficient. Excellent Chairmen, the normal spokesperson for corporate matters, do not necessarily make excellent spokesmen when other issues are under review and coaching of both is essential. Very often tone is as important as content. Certainly the situation should never be under-estimated, mass reporting of one's comments can have far-reaching implications. Generally, humour should not be used, other than by the very experienced.

CASE STUDY 13.1   **Calamity is a four-letter word**

In making a presentation in 1990 to the Institute of Directors, Gerald Ratner, then Chairman of the company which he had successfully built into one of the largest jewellery retailers in the world, was aware that the conference was being video taped and that representatives of all the UK media were present. Wishing to make an effect and impress his comments on the delegates, he humorously compared some of his products to human waste and added that there was more value in a Marks & Spencer prawn sandwich than in some products sold in his shops. The humorous intent was forgotten in the mass reporting of his words which had a calamitous effect on the whole UK chain. The share price tumbled from 177p to 8p and Ratner himself had to give up the Chairmanship and resign as a Director. The combination of the effects of his remark and the UK recession led to the closing of over 350 shops and eventually the change of the company name.

———— KEY TECHNIQUE ————

What may seem innocent fun to us may be taken in a totally different way by our listeners.

The spokesperson must be able to keep calm under pressure, to think swiftly, to appreciate that some answers may be double-edged, that is that either of two responses may be self-critical. To avoid this effect, and to show that their knowledge is sound, the items in the checklist (Fig. 13.2) should be addressed.

1   As comprehensive and complete a brief as possible must be prepared. Organisation data, performance, products, problems, plans and so on, must be available and updated.

2   The point or aim of the interview must be discovered and appropriate responses and statements prepared, particularly if these are likely to be controversial or embarrassing.

3   The spokesperson needs to have total control of the brief, of all facts and of the pre-prepared responses, and to be able to speak knowledgeably concerning the subject matter. Any hesitation, lack of confidence or inadequate knowledge will be communicated to the listener or viewer and create doubt of veracity. In this respect it may be better to admit 'I don't know' rather than to try to 'flannel' through an answer.

4   Three or four simple messages that the organisation wishes to promote, must be developed, possibly with 'changes of direction' sentences, so that if the interviewer leads off in one direction, the spokesperson may be able to return it to the company's preferred message. This approach needs to be controlled since a constant 'refusal' to answer the question may lead to a far more inquisitive or confrontational interview.

5   The spokesperson must be ready for the 'off the cuff' and unrehearsed question deliberately introduced and designed to catch him unawares to lead him to make an unprepared or unwise comment or answer.

6   Above all the spokesperson must be able to keep calm under pressure and/or goading, to be able to think quickly to fend off or deflect aggression and criticism, to retain control, and never to lose their temper.

7   The spokesperson must recognise that most live media interviews last a minute or less and thus it may be possible only to get across two or three authoritative comments. They need to be calm, alert, interested and serious, but never try to be humorous, flustered or flippant. To some extent, particularly on television, the way a message is delivered can be more effective than the content.

8   They should take time to think about the questions, asking for them to be repeated if necessary.

9   False statements should not be allowed to pass unchecked. The record should be corrected.

10 Be positive not defensive. It may be better to 'own up' to a bad performance or event with a promise to 'improve' or rectify, rather than to try to defend an untenable position. The latter alternative will normally display the company in a poor light regardless of the circumstances and the impression will be 'they have learned nothing from the mistake', so nothing will change. This is particularly important when there has been loss, injury or death. It is essential that genuine sympathy is expressed.

Figure 13.2   Media spokesperson checklist

Failing to train, coach or prepare media spokespersons will almost inevitably lead to a situation where, regardless of the rights or wrongs of the situation, the result is that the organisation is shown in a bad light and the reputation of the spokesperson can be called into question.

CASE STUDY 13.2   **Lose your temper – lose the case**

In late 1992 there was considerable media interest in the salaries being paid to Chairmen/Chief Executives of recently privatised water companies who, it was argued, were performing virtually the same job as they had done before privatisation, but were now paying themselves two or three times as much. A number of company Chairmen were interviewed for the BBC TV programme *Panorama*. One such Chairman obviously resented being pressed for an answer regarding his own salary increase to the extent that in trying to get off the set and away from the camera, he became involved in an increasingly heated exchange with the interviewer, all of which was caught on camera.

———— KEY TECHNIQUE ————

There might have been a perfectly acceptable reason for the salary increase, but, if so, this was lost in the argument as was the Chairman's reputation. His staff were at fault for not briefing him adequately on the type of questions that he was likely to be asked, and of providing some logical answers. He should also have been briefed on the possibility of hard questioning, and rehearsed in dealing with intrusive questions with patience and good humour rather than with anger and contempt.

Coaching

It should not be overlooked that the Chairman in Case Study 13.2 lost an ideal opportunity to manipulate the media to his company's advantage. After all, he had been offered a golden opportunity to promote his company on prime-time TV which would otherwise have been prohibitively expensive. Coaching in how to introduce news and reports of laudable developments into the conversation, would also have been valuable. Indeed, since he had overall responsibility for such developments this would have been good ammunition in defence of the salary increase. As it was the overwhelming impression was that the Chairman was unlikely to be worth his salary and any empathy with the viewer was lost.

Pride not hype needed

As Sir John Harvey-Jones, former Chairman of ICI and more widely known for his work in the TV series *Troubleshooter*, once commented, 'a business leader has two priorities, the responsibility to listen and the responsibility to communicate at all times, to be in touch and to remain in touch'. Communication is all about answering questions, including those posed by the media on behalf of the general public, and not evading such questions. As the top person in the organisation one expects to hear and see a display of pride in the accomplishments of the organisation. Indeed, if the Chairman is not going to display such pride, who is? Too often UK organisations are defensive about things that have gone wrong rather than being ready to shout and proclaim things that have gone right. To a certain extent this is a result of the media's predilection with 'bad' news, but it is also a result of organisations not developing a relationship with the media to feed them news stories. In that way, should bad news strike then at least it may be possible to leaven it with some good.

This is not to say that pride in the organisation and its accomplishments must be developed to the extent that the company comes to believe its own hype. 'Hype' is short for hyperbole, 'an exaggerated statement not meant to be taken literally', and companies that come to believe their own hype (that is, something not meant to be wholly believed) are guilty of self-delusion which is inherently dangerous.

CASE STUDY 13.3 **Over hyped**

The company had been built by the Chairman from a tiny one-unit operation into an internationally based, several hundred unit major company, an accomplishment of which everyone could be proud. The report and accounts reflected this history although the shareholder felt that their glossiness and achievement-trumpeting was somewhat 'over the top'. In addition, he could not understand the graphical representation of the company's salient figures in the annual report, and pointed out to the Chairman that the relative size of the bar charts pictorially displaying the company's five-year results overstated the actual for the most recent year by at least 25 per cent. The Chairman dismissed this, referring to the undoubted growth of the company. This the shareholder did not deny but pointed out that this was a prime page in the company's financial document of record, and the impression was misleading. The Chairman was again dismissive and stated that those sort of details were 'left to the report designers'. 'But the Board are responsible,' returned the shareholder, to which the Chairman shrugged his shoulders. The shareholder was so uneasy at the statistics and the Chairman's attitude that he sold his shares in the company. Eighteen months later the company was in serious financial trouble having gone on record with an overstatement of its profits.

——— KEY TECHNIQUE ———

One is prompted to wonder if the company's predeliction for hype after their undoubted early successes precluded them from checking other details.

That hype should be controlled does not mean that everything must be disclosed. There usually needs to be some element of protection of the name and reputation of the company, but if it appears that hype has overtaken reality, expect examination. Whilst total honesty is rare, on occasions candour can have unexpected benefits.

CASE STUDY 13.4 **What we say is what we mean**

The company was facing a hostile takeover bid. Its relationships with the media had been somewhat limited although a few links had been built in the previous six months, whilst its formerly uninformative corporate documentation had been

▶

replaced by genuinely user-friendly and informative reports. At one meeting with the press the Chairman commented, 'I don't suppose you've ever heard of us'. The person responsible for corporate communication initially cringed believing that this unnecessarily denigrated the company as well as the persona of the Chairman. In fact this downbeat beginning laid the foundation of an ongoing impression, that from this company, not a high-flier but one with a solid, dependable record, would be derived truth rather than hype, factual comment rather than promotional material and precise detail rather than innuendo. Conversely, they were being fed a diet of what was eventually shown to be hype, comment and innuendo by the predator.

KEY TECHNIQUE

It took time for the constant repetition of the facts to allay and combat the predator's comments but gradually the press appreciated that the company was telling the truth, backed by facts. In this it was unusual, but this itself tended to create an interest which gained the company considerably more coverage than the size of the bid deserved, as well as substantially enhancing the share price.

During the two months of the bid referred to in Case Study 13.4 the Board of the target company got to know several financial journalists quite well. In this they were assisted by their own corporate public relations advisers who set up media lunches allowing both sides to talk informally of matters of interest. As already noted, when relationships are fostered by the dimension of social activity, greater understanding almost invariably follows. During a bid it is essential that the main arguments are clearly presented in the press since often the battle is lost and won in the pages of the national newspapers rather than in the detailed arguments contained in the predator's and defender's formal documentation. Ensuring that the press reflect the right arguments and points will be achieved more easily if those responsible understand the background that generates such contentions. In turn, this need underpins the desire to cultivate such contacts.

Promoting success

The success of the UK Government's privatisation programme, the awareness, at least until the Stock Market crash in the late 1980s, of the profit that could be made on the Stock Market from investing in public companies, and the number of scandals involving companies and their high-profile Chairmen and Directors in the late 1980s and early 1990s, has combined to move the activities of wealth-creating companies from the financial pages to the general news pages of the national, and even local, press, as well as generating attention from both radio and television. Such companies have plenty of good news and even though an argument amongst high-profile media personnel over the propensity of the media to feature bad rather than good news itself made the national news in early 1993, it can be difficult to gain media attention to good news stories. However, if companies produce news reports or press releases regularly, a database of information is being built by the media which can be used as background for an eventual story.

The local press should not be overlooked as they may be far more willing to feature good news stories than the national press.

The amount of news which is derived by one paper from another should not be under-estimated and the practice can be used to good effect. One problem that emerged as a result of the company's local press day was also turned to good benefit. The local corre-spondent of one national paper telephoned the Chairman in some annoyance at having

---

CASE STUDY 13.5   **It's good news week**

The Chairman and the corporate Public Relations Adviser wished to gain media attention for a new product but felt that it was unlikely to be featured by the national press. Accordingly, they invited six representatives of the local press to their two factories for a comprehensive tour of the new production line, provided in-depth information on the new product and enabled them to ask questions both on the shop floor and in the Boardroom, where luncheon was provided. The Chairman was bullish about the new product, pointing out that not only did it mean increased turnover and profits, but it would also create jobs in an area of high and rising unemployment.

The reporters left with a good selection of samples of the products and an equally good selection of usable quotes. As a result two papers gave the story a full front page coverage and the others also featured it. The national press picked the story up and immediately demanded more information. The Chairman flew to London with samples and photographs and within a matter of days had got what he wanted, national coverage of the product.

---

been excluded from the press day. Apologising and arranging for him to come in separately, the Chairman explained that the company had not been aware of his appointment or location and would be only too pleased to keep him advised of all developments in the future.

CHAPTER FOURTEEN

Meetings under threat

Key learning points

- The manner of discussion initiation tends to generate similar responses, thus temper generates temper, and so on

- Conversely, calmness can, instead of soothing, aggravate temper

- Comprehensive preparation is essential in preparing and delivering presentations

- Advance consideration of other parties' reactions may well enable positive manipulation to be effected

Dealing with aggravation

In many meetings aggravation will be present. Depending on how it is handled, this can either thwart the success of the meeting, and thus its purpose, or be negated so that the meeting's purposes are achieved. To a great extent the control of aggravation tests on how people are handled and in this respect the meeting manipulator, regardless of whether he or she is Chairman or ordinary member, may need to apply some psychology in order to get their way. Most people tend to react in the same way that they are treated, as is summed up in the following children's charter (Fig. 14.1).

Similar precepts apply in meetings. If we approach a meeting in anger then no matter how justified our attitude may be, it may generate a similar attitude from those we meet. Approaching the meeting with calmness but using all the ammunition that could support a loss of temper, may well enable you to out-manoeuvre the opposition and achieve your aim.

The child that lives with:

> *criticism learns to condemn*
> *ridicule learns to be timid*
> *distrust learns to be deceitful*
> *antagonism learns to be hostile.*

Conversely the child that lives with:

> *truth learns justice*
> *knowledge learns wisdom*
> *patience learns to be tolerant*
> *encouragement learns confidence*
> *(source unknown)*

Figure 14.1   The children's charter

CASE STUDY 14.1   Justifiable anger all but loses the point

The Manager was furious that after considerable and protracted delays the agent with whom he was dealing seemed determined to avoid advising either him or his company of matters seriously affecting his company's unit. Twice in four weeks, letters supposedly sent to him had 'gone astray'. The lack of advice thereby wasted time that could have been used to protect the position. He telephoned the agent, and initially receiving an off-hand response which included two or three comments that were incorrect, and a derisory dismissal of the Manager's assertions when it was pointed out that the matter had been dragging on for over two years, unfortunately lost his temper. Then the agent lost his. The ensuing slanging match was terminated after a few irate minutes by both parties slamming down their respective phones. The Manager then cooled down and faxed a letter setting out the evidence of his company's case, including the non-arrival of the two letters, and added copies of the correspondence originated by a colleague of the existing agent, which provided evidence that the matter had indeed been going on for over two years. He concluded his letter by regretting the outburst but hoped the recital of all the matters would show the company's justifiable case. The agent telephoned back with a complete apology, explaining that he was dealing with two companies with the same name and had confused the two in the heat of the moment!

──────── KEY TECHNIQUE ────────

Having cleared the air, the two were able to build a relationship based on understanding, in the interests of which the Manager decided that it might be unwise to press for an explanation for the non-delivery of the two letters that had actually sparked the row!

CASE STUDY 14.2   **Aggravation riles – and loses**

At the doors of the tribunal the consultant was confronted by his opposite number in a fair degree of anger. The papers his opposite number had sent to the tribunal had been mislaid and insufficient copies were available to allow the tribunal to sit. The angry barrister demanded that the consultant provide additional copies so that their case could proceed. The consultant, acting for the defendant, quietly pointed out that as the bundle of papers had been produced by and for the barrister, the onus was on his side to produce replacement copies. During the very heated exchange that followed, the ire of the barrister was countered by the icy calm of the consultant which apparently only served to aggravate the barrister's temper.

The barrister eventually had to arrange for the additional copies or withdraw the case, but was obviously so annoyed by the earlier exchange and the refusal of the consultant to agree to his demands (stated 'as a barrister'), that his grip on the case was insecure and it was lost.

Awkwardness

Despite every endeavour, some situations can generate an adverse reaction which, in order to proceed, needs either to be overcome, changed or, if all else fails, ignored. Unfortunately we can be forced within the context of a meeting to deal with a situation already formed by others. This is not ideal and rather like the fabled answer given to the stranger in Ireland when asking directions to a village – 'Sure, and if I were you I wouldn't start from here' – the option of an alternative start may be attractive but impractical. Thus, we usually have to deal with what we find.

CASE STUDY 14.3   **Totally unprepared**

The consultant had been asked by a client company to visit a small factory situated many miles from its Head Office, to help oversee its closure and the redundancy of 60 to 70 staff. At a week's notice a meeting was set up with the local manager, who had already been briefed on the situation and his own termination package. At the meeting the consultant tactfully tried to discover salient details of the manner of operation, personnel facts and figures and similar data. To all enquiries the local manager stonewalled, replying that he did not have such data available but would discover it and relay it later, or that he needed approval from Head Office before disclosure.

In his initial report to the client, the consultant had to record his surprise at the lack of preparation shown by the local manager given that adequate time had been allowed for the collation of salient facts of the operation, which one would have thought for such a small operation the manager would have at his fingertips. It seemed obvious that the current management was simply not up to the task or had a particular aversion to the present situation.

He suspected that the local manager, despite having a satisfactory termination package, resented the idea of the outsider coming in to help. He thus suggested that a meeting be held at Head Office where the respective roles of manager and consultant were clearly delineated. It was emphasised that the consultant was there to help, not to supplant, but that he had to be given all information in order to be able to help.

Despite considerable efforts to explain and engender the manager's co-operation, he withdrew more and more from the running of the operation and the consultant found that he had to fill the vacuum. At one meeting with the whole

---

workforce there was considerable antipathy directed at the manager who refused to deal with such problems, announced he was going to lunch and left the consultant to try to pacify his staff who by then were threatening to strike.

_____ KEY TECHNIQUE _____

Only by being absolutely open with the employees, and promising regular consultation outside the normal chain of command was the consultant able to avoid the strike that would probably have closed the factory prematurely.

Presentations

The requirement to give presentations to numbers of people in organisations is widespread and often has to be undertaken by those lacking experience. The overriding guideline should be to place oneself in the position of the individual meeting member and to try to assess one's presentation through the recipients' eyes, bearing in mind that all distractions should be avoided.

CASE STUDY 14.4 **Keys lock out attention**

The Chairman was used to commanding attention and experienced in chairing and speaking at board meetings. He was not, however, used to speaking to a conference and when the management of the company were gathered together at such a conference, at which he had to give the keynote presentation, he was very nervous. This nervousness manifested itself in a habit of which he was entirely unaware. He kept his left hand in his trouser pocket constantly fingering a set of keys. The sound of these keys jingling eventually became such a distraction to the audience that the impact of his keynote address was lost. During the first coffee break the discussion was more about the keys than about the content!

──────── KEY TECHNIQUE ────────

Every distraction, or potential distraction, should be avoided to ensure the effectiveness of the presentation.

Such anti-social behaviour is not restricted to the speaker. Often it emanates from the audience. Regardless of its source it can be very disturbing, both to the other delegates whose attention will be distracted and to the speaker who may find his or her own attention wandering and the calibre of the presentation itself impaired. Such anti-social behaviour can include talking to another delegate, humming or tapping a pencil. The difficulty is that often the person concerned is virtually unaware of the action or of the effect it is having, particularly if the presentation scenario is new to them. If a break is near then it may be acceptable to wait until the break before quietly and tactfully explaining to the delegate that the action is causing a problem. Alternatively, it may be necessary to break into the programme with a tactfully worded request to desist.

CASE STUDY 14.5   **Avoiding distractions**

At a seminar with around 40 delegates, two from the same organisation, sitting in the front row, chatted incessantly and it was obvious to the speaker that, although he was not affected too badly, delegates were finding it difficult to concentrate. In inviting questions, the speaker positioned himself so that the chatterers were directly between him and a questioner. He was then able to say to the questioner, 'I'm sorry, I can't hear you,' and then to the chatterers, 'I'm sorry, but could you break off your conversation? I can't hear the question which may affect the point you are discussing.' This was followed up by a tactful word in the next break.

The meeting instigator must control, and be seen to control, the meeting with firmness, tact and humour. The guidelines in Fig. 14.2 should be borne in mind.

1 Stand in a relaxed manner. In this way it is physically easy to speak and you command attention.

2 Present without a jacket or coat. Whilst in some instances this may be inappropriate, normally it will indicate to the delegates that you are prepared to get down to business.

3 Make eye contact with delegates. Whilst this can be difficult with more than, say, 40 delegates, eye contact creates rapport and enables the speaker to check receptivity. If eyes become glazed or puzzled the speaker can recap and re-explain, whilst if they become closed, an attention gainer may be needed.

4 Humour should be used with discretion. Making delegates laugh both relaxes them and makes them inhale oxygen which restores their attention and prevents drowsiness. Conversely, too much laughter can belittle the presentation.

5 Avoid distractions, both personal and within the room. Windows should be masked if they open on to an area which can provide distractions. The meeting room should not have a telephone, whilst visitors and interruptions, including noise from surrounding areas, should be avoided.

6 Ensure that the speaker can see all the audience and that the audience can all see the speaker. Provide notes so that the audience only has to write its own amplifying comments.

7 Simplicity should be the watchword. Jargon should be avoided or at least explained. Speaker's notes should be prepared and arranged in order so that the presentation proceeds smoothly. Similarly, all aids and handouts should also be arranged in order.

8 With smaller groups, if the speaker distributes handouts of particular importance by hand during the session, this can aid rapport. Movement attracts attention.

9 Logical progression of content is essential, with appropriate links between subjects. If the order of content is disrelated, the audience may become confused, and if they are confused their attention will wander. Ease of familiarity with the subject matter is all important.

10 Use visual aids to complement the presentation and to encourage attentiveness. All equipment, computer display, video, slide projector, overhead projector, and so on, should be checked out and alternatives made available so that if there is a failure the disruption can be minimised. If all else fails there should always be a flip chart. Don't overuse such equipment however – it should complement not overcome the content.

11 Invite questions and comments. Again this will aid rapport and enable the speaker to check that the points have been taken on board by the meeting members. Answer questions as honestly as possible and if asked a question to which you do not know the answer, say so and promise to get back to the questioner having checked the point out.

12 In larger groups, recognise that many delegates will be inhibited from posing questions verbally – either through a fear of speaking publicly or through a fear that the question will be regarded as 'silly'. In these circumstances, encourage the use of written questions, providing pads for the purpose. It can also help to stress that the 'silliest' question is the one that isn't asked!

Figure 14.2   Guidelines for successful presentations

CASE STUDY 14.6   **Using the expert delegates**

The speakers at the presentation were concerned that two delegates were very experienced in the subject under consideration. To avoid being challenged or corrected by them, the speakers regularly invited their comments as if they were part of the presentation team. In this way animosity was avoided and used. The skill of the delegates was recognised and channelled to help all involved rather than being ignored and suppressed which could lead to animosity. People do like to be recognised.

Bad news

There is no easy or best way of communicating bad news. There are, unfortunately, constant examples of bad ways of dealing with such matters. People are not fools and resent being treated other than as responsible adults. Whilst they may not welcome bad news, most are mature enough to know that everything cannot be sweetness and light all the time. Treating people like responsible adults, outlining the situation that has resulted in the decision and explaining the bad news and its implications will often aid acceptance. Ignoring human respect tends to lead to trouble.

CASE STUDY 14.7   **Handled well ...**

The Group had decided that the continuation of production at the local factory was untenable and had received an offer, which it wished to accept, for part of the productive capacity. The decision would mean the redundancy of the workforce in an area where unemployment was already high and the likelihood of the workforce finding alternative jobs was remote. The Group management decided to make a presentation of the position to the staff and several members travelled over 300 miles to hold a meeting with all the employees.

    The meeting pulled no punches, explained the trading position, explained the proposal to sell part of the product list, outlined the redundancy terms, promised

---

that within 48 hours each person would be seen individually (which they were) and introduced a Director who would work with them, if they wished, to try to find alternative work for them in the area.

Whilst shocked, and, in some cases emotional, the employees accepted the position, asked a number of relevant and useful questions, thanked the Directors for making such a long journey to see them, and even sympathised with them for having to deal such a nasty decision and announcement!

———— KEY TECHNIQUE: ————

Treating people with respect and appreciating their likely reactions can defuse apparently contentious meetings.

The face-to-face meeting, and the trouble taken to make it so, was not merely altruistic. The Group genuinely believed that its employees were its greatest assets and tried to put people first whenever possible, not just because it seemed the right thing to do, the 'do as you would be done by' principle, but because there were sound business reasons for so doing. People work and perform best when they work willingly and with good motivation. The redundancy period faced in the local factory was quite long, over six months in some cases. During that time production was still required and the motivation of the workforce was essential. If the goodwill generated by the visit, and later repeat visits, and the outplacement facility, had been absent, it was hardly likely that output, which actually achieved record levels in the period, would have even been maintained. The company also had a reputation to preserve in the area where its goods would continue to be available.

CASE STUDY 14.8   **... and not so well**

Conversely, when a major public company had to implement a considerable redundancy programme it did so by means of notices posted on boards. There was no cohesion regarding the announcement, nor any consistency regarding the posting of the notices as not all the units affected received a copy. The information the notices contained was incomplete, there was no consultation with either union, which was legally required, or with non-union employees. A damaging strike was the immediate reaction.

———— KEY TECHNIQUE: ————

In contrast to Case Study 14.7, ignoring people's views and not granting them respect can *only* aggravate a difficult situation.

Interviews

The successful interview is one where both parties attending the meeting discover sufficient information about the other to enable them to make an objective decision regarding the possibility of them having a successful relationship should the applicant be appointed. All too often, however, those responsible for recruitment regard the interview as a one-sided process and frame the interview to answer only the question: 'is this person likely to be right for the position?' This overlooks the equally important question that must be asked by the applicant: 'is this organisation likely to be right for me?' The strengths of the two parties are unequal. The applicant is alone and has far more at stake than the organisation. Thus the second question could be the more important of the two. Operating an interview meeting under this misconception, that is ignoring or negating the legitimate interests of the applicant, can swiftly lead to a situation where the best is unlikely to be obtained from the interview.

CASE STUDY 14.9   **Off-putting**

Having completed the initial interview and been offered a further short-list interview for a senior job in the organisation, the applicant was staggered to find that all six short-listed candidates had been asked to attend at the same time. Interviews were planned to take place consecutively and all candidates were expected to wait until the last had been completed when a decision would be announced. The first interview took 50 minutes and with the pause between interviews, and a gap for lunch the applicant calculated the sequence was likely to last around six to seven hours.

One candidate made the point to the receptionist that this method of conducting the selection had not been explained in the letter of invitation, and he found the suggestion that all candidates should waste several hours unacceptable. As presumably this was an indication of the way the organisation wished to operate, he decided that its ethos was not in tune with his and withdrew from the selection process, to be followed by two other candidates.

——— KEY TECHNIQUE ———

If candidates find themselves patronised, as was the impression, if not the intent, or their goodwill is abused, or their interests simply ignored, as in Case Study 14.9, they are hardly likely to be endeared to the system and may cause a backlash not in the interests of the organisation, particularly if that attitude then receives publicity.

Discipline

The disciplinary procedure provides countless opportunities for confrontation within meetings. To try to minimise this, those instituting such meetings need to prepare with great care, with nothing left to chance. Every fact should be checked and every accusation examined to ensure that they are fair, well-founded and well-evidenced. Further, the rules of natural justice, under which disciplinary hearings should be conducted, require that the defendant is given every opportunity to defend himself, provide counter-evidence, call witnesses and plead any mitigating circumstances. It should never be forgotten that the primary purpose of the disciplinary procedure is to try to convince the offender of the need to abide by the way of doing things required by his employer, that is its positive purpose. It is not just a means of gathering evidence to be used to construct a case for dismissal and to defend a future tribunal case, which can be termed its negative purpose.

Appraisal

An appraisal should be an objective review of an employee's work by their manager, and possibly by their higher manager. Inevitably it also provides an opportunity for dissent and disagreement. To overcome or avoid this an individual job description agreed by each employee should be prepared. This should avoid many of the demarcation 'that's not my job' arguments, whilst the addition of 'measures of performance' against each item on the job description itself will turn the questions of capability into an objective discussion of how near the attainment of the measures the employee came. In this way the appraisal interview should be set up to encourage a positive discussion, avoiding some of the 'yes you did' 'no I didn't' arguments.

Takeover

There is little in the business environment that can match a hostile takeover battle for heated argument, dissent, and aggravation. Whilst some of such comment may be moderated to tones suitable for print, ultimately the bid is all about the predator's belief that their talent to run the target company is better than that of the incumbent management, and vice versa, which tends to raise tempers. It is no part of this book to discuss takeovers in general, although it is worth noting that research indicates that only relatively few hostile takeovers actually work. Within the context of the bid and defence, there are opportunities for countless meetings when extra caution and awareness may be essential.

CASE STUDY 14.10   **Dirty work in the car park**

The company defending a bid had been approached by a contact who stated that he had information that would be of use in the defence. He also stated that he had evidence that the company's offices were bugged and refused to discuss the information inside the building. Accordingly the Chairman, Secretary and contact moved to the car park. The Secretary asked whether the information was readily available from other sources and was told that it was unlikely as it had been obtained via a possibly illegal method. The Secretary advised the Chairman to withdraw from the meeting before the information was discussed. This would enable the Chairman to deny, if questioned, whether he knew anything of the source of the information. The information thus sourced somehow found its way into the papers where it helped firm up a few doubtful shareholders in favour of the defending company. In some cases being ignorant of some facts can be very valuable.

———— KEY TECHNIQUE ————

It is not just bugging devices that enable conversations to be overheard. I was once carrying on a telephone meeting with the works managers of two of the company's factories. I was having difficulty convincing them that some proposals they were suggesting were in breach of employment law, when to the surprise of all of us, the voice of the Managing Director was heard telling my two colleagues that they were wrong. Whilst it was pleasant to have my own view confirmed, it was disconcerting to discover that the MD could listen to all internal telephone conversations. From then on telephone meetings tended to be avoided in favour of the face-to-face variety which was probably beneficial in every way!

CHAPTER FIFTEEN

Formal meetings

Key learning points

- Formal meetings require guidelines and requirements formulated and promulgated

- Preparation is essential and support, in the face of opposition, may need to be canvassed

- Providing a Chairman's brief can aid the meeting being manipulated to the ends required

- 'Planted' questions can be used to bring into the open any points required for closer examination

Legal meetings

Various organisations are required to hold meetings, particularly with their owners or creditors, at certain times and to consider at those meetings required business. Because of this external requirement such meetings can be regarded as something of a chore by those responsible for them. This can result in insufficient preparation being given to the meetings, but since they often cover matters in the public interest, this can backfire and cause the company embarrassment. To avoid such a possibility, preparation and research is required. If properly completed and prepared, a potentially damaging incident can be manipulated into good public relations.

CASE STUDY 15.1 **Gaining the advantage**

At an Annual General Meeting of one of the UK's premier high street retailers, a customer/shareholder wanted to know why it was impossible to buy swimwear at one of the chain's seaside resort shops. The Chairman dealt with the question with good humour explaining that the computerised stock system had by accident deleted the particular unit from stock allocation but that rectification of the error was currently taking place.

———— KEY TECHNIQUE ————

By having information available and dealing with the question with both good humour and sympathy, and avoiding any defensive reaction, the Chairman of the meeting was able to avoid the implied criticism and gain good public relations material when the matter was reported in a number of national papers the following day.

The reaction outlined in Case Study 15.1 can only occur when the Chairman has been properly briefed on what is required for the meeting, and what bombshells he may have to defuse or combat. He is prepared to be honest and above all handles the situation positively. In this respect, accepting that 'we made a mistake' can win respect and plaudits provided, of course, it doesn't happen too often. Conversely, trying to defend an impossible position, which many attempt and usually fail, reflects poorly on both speaker and organisation.

Such general meetings, particularly those of listed companies, can be the sole occasion in the year when the corporate entity is 'on display' and for that reason, they need careful planning to ensure that the company is seen in as advantageous a light as possible. Whether the meeting is to be such a showcase, or is regarded more as a chore, it needs adequate preparation, either as part of the year-end activities or as a separate occasion in its own right. The items set out in the checklist in Fig. 15.1 should serve as a draft for all meetings of this nature.

Briefing the Chairman

So that the Chairman can control and manipulate the meeting as wished, it is advisable to prepare well in advance. The actual matters to be considered will vary according to the requirements of the particular meeting but generally, the more preparation work is completed in advance of the meeting then the more smoothly the meeting should progress. In many respects this may require advance knowledge of possible contentious issues.

CASE STUDY 15.2   **Defensive measures**

It is not simply administrative matters that require attention so that top directors can be briefed, high profile embarassments can be avoided provided those responsible are alert.

Under Company Law many companies require a proportion of their Board of Directors to retire each year and seek re-election at the discretion of the shareholders attending their Annual General Meeting. After a disastrous trading period the Chief Executive Director of one company realised that he was due to retire and seek re-election at the forthcoming AGM.

Unwilling to run the risk of failing to be re-elected and the consequent considerable embarassment at the end of a distinguished career, he tendered his resignation before the meeting was held.

General meeting checklist

1 Prepare list/timetable of all items needing to be addressed.

2 Allocate items to named executives.

Item	Responsibility
Decide date and time	Board
Visit venue, check facilities	Company Secretary
Book venue (6/12 months ahead)	,,

Check
- room and overflow facility — Executive responsible
- air conditioning/ventilation — ,,
- acoustics/amplification — ,,
- accommodation including catering/toilet facilities — ,,
- notice boards/room directions — ,,
- tables for signing in — ,,

If product/photo display required
- display tables/pin or felt boards — ,,

Stipulate
- timetable for arrivals — ,,
- serving tea/coffee — ,,
- lunch (if required) — ,,
- likely departure — ,,

Delegate items to staff, e.g.
- greeting arrivals — ,,
- ensuring arrivals sign in — ,,
- ushering to seats — ,,
- care of registers and proxies — ,,
- act as teller (in event of poll) — ,,
- care of statutory books, service,contracts, minute book — ,,
- liaison with catering — ,,
- arranging and checking arrival of proposers/seconders, and arranging substitutions in event of absence — ,,
- display of products/tour of premises — ,,
- preparation of Chairman's crib (i.e. a script to cover each part of the meeting) — ,,
- preparation of and answers to awkward questions — ,,
- briefing on preparations, likely problems, etc — ,,
- preparation of a complete meeting scenario, for Board and advisers — ,,

Figure 15.1   Public or formal meeting checklist

- liaison with auditors, solicitors, brokers, public
  relations and, through them, media representatives   ,,
- guests' transport arrangements   ,,

3 Ensure all appointed executives understand requirements. Newcomers to the task should be fully briefed in the requirements and their progress checked regularly. Those who have not attended such a meeting previously should be sent to one.

4 Re-check preparations one month prior to event as it is essential that this public showing of the company is seen to be smooth and efficient. It will, after all, be a reflection of how the company operates.

5 Consider style/content to be adopted with Chairman/Board. Some organisations make these meetings less formal, even advertising that members of the Board will be available before or after the meeting for individual discussion.

6 Coach spokespersons in handling the media and any parties likely to be critical of the organisation. This is particularly important if dealing with hostile or critical questioning. Unless well-prepared and well-briefed for this type of examination, reputations, of both person and company, can be irreparably damaged and unnecessarily bad impressions provided.

7 Prepare for hostility as follows:

- Identify source and extent of support and of opposition.
- Ensure that 'hostiles' have a right of attendance and consider exclusion if not.
- If time allows, consider the possibility of a private meeting to avoid public confrontation.
- Monitor arrivals, arrange for security forces to be nearby to deal with any physical disruption.
- Canvass support/proxies sufficient to ensure overcoming any potential opposition.
- Prepare a list of the questions least wished to be asked, and a crib of suitable answers. This may require the convening of a brainstorming session attended by corporate lawyers, merchant bankers, auditors, and so on, as well as the Board and Secretary, at which every aspect of the company's record is investigated and the worst questions, and more importantly some reliable answers, are framed. The answers need to be well-rehearsed by those responsible for speaking at the meeting. It should be noted that in this respect it will provide a better impression of the company if such questions are 'farmed out' to various members of the Board. This will give an impression of a multi-member 'team' being in control rather than a sole 'dictator'.
- Consider approaching 'friendly' shareholders with a view to gaining their agreement to ask prepared questions which allow the Board to provide answers showing the company in a reasonably good light. This emulates the Government 'planting' questions to the Prime Minister in his twice weekly question session in the House of Commons.
- Brief media contacts and provide media-trained spokespersons to answer follow-up queries.
- If the hostile wishes to make a point he/she should be allowed such a courtesy answering the points made as far as possible and offering subsequent discussions if this is feasible.

Figure 15.1   Continued

Chairman's crib for XXth Annual General Meeting

At [*time*] call meeting to order. Ladies and Gentlemen I welcome you to the XXth AGM of .... Ltd/plc. May I commence the formal proceedings, following which you will be able to meet members of the Board and other executives and chat informally over some refreshments which we have requested. We have, as you can see around you, provided displays of our products and services. The Notice of this meeting was dispatched to all members of the Company on [*date*] and I will ask the Secretary to read it.

[*Secretary reads notice*]

The first item on the agenda concerns the consideration of the Directors' Report with the report and accounts for the [*twelve*] months ended [*date*]. Those accounts and the balance sheet as at that date have been audited by your Auditor Messrs [*name*] and I request Mr [*name a partner*] of that firm of registered auditors to deliver the Audit Report.

[*Auditor reads report*]

May I propose that the Report of the Directors, together with the annexed statement of the Company's accounts for the [*twelve*] months ended and the Balance Sheet as at that date duly audited be now received, approved and adopted. Has anyone any questions or comment? [*Pause*] [*If questions are raised it will be necessary to deal with them or if they are of a technical/financial nature pass them to Finance Director to handle.*]
As part of that proposal may I also propose that a final dividend of [*amount*] per cent or [*amount*] pence per share on the Ordinary shares of the Company payable on [*date*] be now declared for the [twelve] months ended [date]. I call upon [name] to second that proposal.
All those in favour please raise your hands. [*Pause*] Anyone against? [*Pause*] [*Assess and declare the result.*]

I therefore declare the motion carried.

Item 2 concerns the re-election of the retiring Director(s). The director(s) retiring by rotation is/are [*name(s)*] and I have much pleasure in proposing that [name] be and he hereby is re-elected a Director of the Company. I will ask [*name*] to second that proposal.

All those in favour [*pause*] and against. [*Pause*] [*Declare the result.*] I declare Mr [*name*] duly re-elected a Director of the Company.

[*NB If more than one Director retires by rotation separate proposals are required for each unless a proposal to deal with all such re-elections as a single entity has been passed. Proposals may also be needed to re-elect Directors who have been appointed since the previous AGM. Re-elected Directors may wish to express their thanks to the meeting.*]

Item 3 concerns the re-election of Messrs [*auditors*] as Auditors of the Company and I call upon Mr [*name*] to propose that resolution and Mr [*name*] to second it.

All those in favour. [*Pause*] Anyone against? [*pause*] [*Declare result.*]

Item 4 authorises the Directors to fix the remuneration of the Auditors and I will ask Mr [*name*] to propose that resolution and Mr [*name*] to second it.

Figure 15.2   Chairman's crib – Ordinary General Meeting

All those in favour. [*Pause*] Anyone against? [*Pause*] [*Declare the result.*]

Is there any other ordinary business for consideration?

[*Note: other than the proposal of a vote of thanks to the Chairman and/or Board it is unlikely that anything else can be discussed by the meeting since notice of such business will not have been given.*]

I therefore declare this XXth AGM closed. Thank you.

Figure 15.2   Continued

Figure 15.2 deals with a straightforward General Meeting and provides the Chairman with what should be an adequate script for a non-contentious meeting. General Meetings are not always so harmonious however.

CASE STUDY 15.3   **Hanson is as Hanson does**

When the successful UK company Hanson wished to change its constitution so that the matters that could be raised publicly by individual shareholders at its Annual General Meeting would be somewhat curtailed. It quickly became obvious that there was considerable antipathy and adverse reaction to this suggestion and the meeting held to consider the changes could, as a result, be very stormy. As a result of such an anticipated response the proposals were dropped by the company. Whilst the company might well have won, the adverse publicity and antipathy of many of its shareholders was presumably felt to be too high a price.

Out-guessing the opposition

Trying to guess the opposition's questions and tactics is an essential ingredient in manipulating the meeting to achieve one's own ends. This is not something that can be left to chance or to the last minute. It too requires careful consideration and planning, as has been recommended for the whole of such a meeting.

Before the meeting covered by the crib, a shortened version of which appears as Fig. 15.3, the Chairman and the Secretary took considerable time to try to assess the possible reactions of the opposition and any tactics that could be employed by them to sway the meeting. Taking time to identify all the angles in advance enables consideration of a number of alternatives in order to determine which is most likely to succeed in the easiest way. Thus Mr K's request for additional business was technically out of time, but fighting this issue would have been a major distraction to the company as he could simply have requested the convening of another general meeting. Allowing it to go through and be considered, knowing that at the end of the day it could be voted down by the current Board's supporters was a far more pragmatic (and manipulative) approach.

What is required is an objective analysis of the questions the Board would most want NOT to be asked – and, of course, some acceptable and convincing answers. Whilst giving rehearsed answers may make the meeting appear as somewhat orchestrated – at least it will give the impression of preparedness.

Preparing for opposition

If antipathy/hostility is expected, those responsible for the meeting might consider the following:

1 Identify the source of the dissent and ensure they have a right to attend the meeting. If not, barring access may be feasible.

2 Monitor arrivals and arrange for security forces to be nearby to deal with any physical disruption – if, for example, the barring in 1) above generates this.

3 Canvass proxies from those unable to be present, or support from those who will be present sufficient to ensure overcoming any potential opposition.

4 Brief the directors concerned of the source of the problem(s) and the steps taken to control/deal with it.

5 Brief tame media contacts and provide media trained spokesman to answer follow up queries.

6 If the hostile member, with a right to be present, wishes to make a point, he should be allowed such a courtesy.

7 The Chairman should answer points made as far as possible and may be able to circumvent the desire for publicity that raising the matter in the meeting provides, by offering subsequent discussions outside the meeting.

Those responsible for the meeting have a duty to those attending to try and ensure the meeting proceeds as smoothly and efficiently as possible.

Chairman's crib for meeting anticipating opposition

[NB Mr Chairman, I have assumed that voting will be by show of hands in which case a simple majority of hands carries the resolution – i.e. each shareholder has one vote. It is, however, possible under the Articles for any shareholder to demand a poll in which case the meeting must be suspended whilst we conduct a poll in which the number of shares held decides the outcome. If a poll is demanded we also need to appoint tellers.]

Call meeting to order at 12 noon.

Chairman: Ladies and gentlemen, my name is [x]. At a meeting held on 4th February, the Board requested me to assume the role of Chairman. This Extra-ordinary General Meeting was convened by the Board by a notice issued on 28th January which I propose we take as read – does anyone object to that? [Pause – assuming no objection.]

Subsequently, a shareholder holding in excess of 10 per cent of the shares requested that a further item of business be considered at this meeting and we shall deal with that as resolution Number 8. Since the first item on the Agenda concerns myself I shall vacate the chair and ask Mr Y to deal with this item.

Y: Thank you Mr Chairman. Ladies and gentlemen, as you will see the first item on the Agenda concerns the proposal to confirm the appointment of Mr X as Chairman. Technically neither this nor items 2 and 3 need be dealt with at a General Meeting, but in view of the financial situation of the Company and the dissent that has prefaced this meeting, it was thought this would be advisable. Accordingly I would like to propose that Mr X's appointment as Chairman of the Board be and it hereby is confirmed. Do I have a seconder?

All those in favour? Anyone against? I declare the motion carried and hand the meeting back to the Chairman.

Chairman: Thank you. At the meeting which appointed myself as Chairman, a majority of the Directors also appointed Z as Managing Director in succession to K. I would now like to propose that Z's appointment as Managing Director be and it hereby is confirmed. Do I have a seconder?

All those in favour? Anyone against? I declare the motion carried. [Note: We can expect K and one or two supporters to vote against this, but support I have already canvassed is overwhelming.]

The next two items on the Agenda concern the creation of additional share capital which is necessary so that the major restructuring of the Company on which we have been working for some weeks can take place. Copies of the formal resolution which must be filed with the Registrar of Companies have been given to you and I would now like to propose that:

Figure 15.3   Draft Chairman's crib

The share capital of the Company be increased from £10 000 to £2 000 000 by the creation of:

a) 990 000 new ordinary shares of £1 each ranking in all respects *pari passu* with the 10 000 existing ordinary shares of £1 of the company, and

b) the creation of 1 000 000 Preference Shares of £1.

Do I have a seconder? All those in favour? Anyone against? I therefore declare that resolution carried.

The shareholders are required to appoint Auditors for the Company, and although the Board originally requested ABC to act as auditors, a role they carried out until the end of 1997, it was felt more advisable to appoint auditors located nearer to the Company. As part of the investigation carried out by Mr Z, an audit to 2nd November 1998 was completed by Messrs DEF, and I now propose that Messrs DEF be and they hereby are appointed Auditors of the Company until the conclusion of the first Annual General Meeting which we must hold within the next few weeks.

Do I have a seconder? All those in favour? Anyone against? I declare that resolution carried.

The next item concerns the restructuring of the Company and the strategy for the next two years, details of which are included in a report from Mr Z, copies of which have been sent to you. This report, and the audit report contained within it, were prepared very urgently, virtually without notice, and within a very short time span.

Inevitably, some shortcuts have needed to be taken and the Board is aware that there are a number of errors which need to be rectified at an operational level. We are asking today for shareholder approval in principle to the plan which requires, amongst other things, the conversion of shareholder loans which we will deal with in a moment.

I would like you to confirm your acceptance of this plan with those comments in mind, and without discussion since the matter is so urgent we need to move to the next item. However, if any shareholder does wish to make any comments …

[*You will have to play this by ear*]

The next item concerns the conversion of loans made by us all to the Company as part of the shareholding investment. Although it may be arguable that it is permissible for such loans to be counted as shareholder investments, the advice that the Board now has, including that from its new Auditors, is that these loans do not constitute shareholder investments and that the Company is insolvent. We need everyone to agree today to convert these loans into ordinary shares. Unless this is done, we cannot see that new money can flow into the Company which is the only way the Company can survive beyond next week. Thus the Directors take the view that it is a choice of converting loans into shares or our needing to put the Company into receivership. If the loans are not converted your investment is lost, whereas if they are

Figure 15.3   Continued

converted, there is a chance of saving the Company and thus your investment. This is not something on which we can vote since it must be an individual decision, although one where everyone's investment rests on everyone agreeing to convert.

Any comments?

[*Again you will have to play it by ear. I have forms that will enable shareholders to either (a) convert loans into ordinary shares, or (b) convert some loans into ordinary shares and some into preference shares, or (c) invest new money in ordinary shares and/or preference shares. You will need to put pressure on shareholders to try to ensure they sign one of the forms.*]

The last item concerns a request made by Mr K for an alteration to the Articles. Before we can consider the item itself, which we have set out on the handout, you will note that the short notice given in respect of this item needs to be agreed. The Board think it would be advisable for everyone to agree to consider the item and thus I would propose that resolution (b) be considered by the meeting notwithstanding that short notice was given.

Those in favour? Any against? I declare the motion carried in which case we may now deal with the proposal put forward by Mr K that the Articles of Association be changed as set out in the wording of the resolution. Mr K, do you wish to make any comments regarding this resolution? Please be brief as the state of the Company needs all our urgent work.

[*Again you will have to play it by ear but at the end of any discussion, you will need to put it to the vote – those in favour, those against, and declare the result. I suppose it is just possible that we might have a demand for a poll here.*]

That concludes the business of this Extra-ordinary General Meeting. May I thank you for attending.

Figure 15.3   Continued

_____ KEY TECHNIQUE _____

This crib was devised for an Extra-ordinary General Meeting of a company in financial trouble. It tried to anticipate all possible reactions, particularly from Mr K, the former Managing Director, who previously had been removed from office by the Board. It also tried to provide guidance to the Chairman [shown in square brackets] as well as a draft script for him. Opposition was anticipated from Mr K since, as a continuing shareholder he had a right to attend the meetings and had requested additional business be considered. Rather than fight the business, the Board allowed it to be included knowing they could then vote it down.

Large meetings = lack of consensus

Inherent in the convening of public meetings, such as the instances set out above, is the recognition that not all those entitled to attend will do so. Indeed, in many instances of public companies (some with in excess of 2 million shareholders) it would be virtually impossible to hold the meeting if everyone did attend! The fact that many cannot or will not attend is overcome by the expedient of allowing them to vote by proxy, that is appointing someone else, usually the Chairman of the meeting, to vote for them. Thus their votes become amalgamated. It is unlikely that every member will agree with the business being proposed and that there may need to be a vote with the majority usually prevailing. This leaves the minority in the situation where they either 'like it or lump it'. Where those concerned are shareholders this is fairly easily rectified, as they will usually have the option of simply selling their shares. Where the minority is a faction of a Board of Directors or a committee, the situation of the minority needs close re-examination. Attempting to manipulate large meetings can be difficult and requires considerable planning, as well as canvassing of support.

Losing out

It is a fact of life that some meeting members seem to delight in being in opposition even when heavily outnumbered. In formal meetings such a device may be used in order to gain 'cause' publicity. Thus public company meetings have been disrupted by anti-apartheid, anti-blood sports, environmental and animal rights movements amongst others. Rehearsing for such interruptions and having available answers to questions likely to be posed is essential, even though the subject matter may be incidental to the point of the meeting. Failure to prepare for this kind of demonstration hands the initiative to the opposition who succeed in their determination to manipulate the meeting.

In less public arenas opposition may be more concerned to embarrass or defeat particular meeting members or even the Chairman. If this movement gains support then it is arguable that the opposition has become the lead party. Certainly if the Chairman is always in the minority in terms of the results of business considered, it is difficult to see how he can continue in his position. If, despite all his testing of support, endeavouring to neutralise weak opposition and overcome strong opposition, he cannot muster support for business which he supports then his own position is virtually untenable.

Conclusion

As members of the human race, it is impossible for us to opt out of the meeting scenario. Human beings are communicative beings and, hermits apart, in every aspect of our lives we are forced to meet and interface with others of our species. Examination of the process by which we carry on this essential interface tends to suggest that often such meetings occur without our fully anticipating sufficiently all the possible outcomes. In addition, if we do not determine and remember our preferred solution at all times, despite aggravation, deliberate deviation from the subject, filibustering, and so on, we will almost certainly not get what we want when we want. Before becoming involved in a meeting, whether it be an informal one-to-one or a more or less formal multi-member interface, it is essential to determine our desired result, and, since we tend not always to be able to achieve this, our fall-back position. The latter should be the result with which we are prepared to live even though it is not our ideal.

Once we have assessed these two positions, we then need to study our opponent and determine their two equivalent positions. If these are likely to coincide with ours, progress can be made. Normally however, it is unlikely that the two or more interests will coincide. Although it may be possible to apply pressure to win the day, this will not always be effective. Indeed, it may not be the best solution in the long run, as the strength of relative positions tends to run in cycles and opponents who have been forced to concede more than they feel fair may be able to take revenge when the terms move in their favour. A more subtle means of achieving our ends may then be advantageous. The best way to win at meetings may be to do so without making it obvious that the opponent has lost. Gentle manipulation using devices such as those outlined here, may be the best way to ensure that you get what you want when you want.

Index